The Autobiography
of
An Old Drifter

by

PERCY M. CLARK

Rhodesiana Reprint Library
Volume Twenty-six

Facsimile reproduction of the
1936 edition, with new Publishers'
Introduction

BOOKS OF RHODESIA
BULAWAYO 1972

BOOKS OF RHODESIA PUBLISHING CO. (PVT.) LTD.
P.O. Box 1994 Bulawayo

Publishers of Rhodesiana Reprints
and New Rhodesian Literary Works.

PRINTED IN RHODESIA BY MARDON PRINTERS (PVT.) LTD., BULAWAYO.

RE-PUBLICATION of this book has been made possible by the assistance of two Rhodesians of a Pioneer family whose wish it is that it be

dedicated to

THE RHODESIA PIONEERS' AND EARLY SETTLERS' SOCIETY

to honour the men and women who pioneered Rhodesia, and to promote a wider interest in the country's history.

The publishers gratefully acknowledge this help and have pleasure in making this out-of-print Rhodesiana work available to the public of Rhodesia through this Books of Rhodesia series.

PUBLISHERS' INTRODUCTION

EVER since their discovery by David Livingstone in 1855, the Victoria Falls have attracted people from every part of the world but none stayed as long as Percy Clark whose renowned curio shop has had almost as many visitors as the Falls themselves. A great deal of Zambesi water has flowed under the gracefully arched bridge since he arrived there on 8th May 1903 to settle; in fact, as the first permanent resident he preceded the building of the bridge.

In those early days, the 'port of entry' from Southern Rhodesia to North-Western Rhodesia was the 'Old Drift', some five miles above the Falls. The small settlement there comprised two or three small trading stores on the river bank and about a dozen white men, among them Percy Clark, who were proud to be known as 'Old Drifters'. It was a fever-ridden spot and in one rainy season eleven of them succumbed to malaria and blackwater fever. A few graves on the north bank are the only reminders of this early commercial enterprise.

In 1904 the railway reached the Victoria Falls and on 12th September the bridge was officially opened, heralding the commencement of Rhodesia's tourist industry. Percy Clark had foreseen the opportunities which the coming of the railway would bring, and in advance of its arrival he had erected a hut near the site of the future station and hotel. This was the beginning of his curio and photographic business which is still in existence. It is now run by his son, Victor, who was born in 1909.

Percy Clark was born in Cambridge in 1874. At nine he was a chorister at St. Peter's, the oldest of the Cambridge Colleges. His first job, on leaving school, was in the laboratory of the public analyst. He was later an assistant at the University laboratories; however, a new interest in photography, and the toss of a coin, decided his future career as a professional photographer. After an apprenticeship with several leading firms, including a Court photographer in Kensington, he came to Bulawayo to open a photographic department for a local chemist.

Bulawayo at the turn of the century was a tin town frequently smothered by 'dust devils'. One of his earliest assignments was to photograph Rhodes laying the foundation stone of the Drill Hall where, not many months later, he took pictures of his lying-in-state and burial at the Matopos. In about 1902 he went into business on his own, travelling the country taking pictures at mines. His first journey to the Victoria Falls was by construction train to the railhead, then by wagon to Wankie colliery, and from there on foot accompanied by 18 porters. It took over two weeks.

Although he was not the first to photograph the Falls—Chapman in company with Baines took the first pictures in 1862— no one has caught as many of the river's moods and aspects as he. He once made a study of the sketches of the Falls by Livingstone, Baines and others, and produced comparative photographs taken at the same time of day and month of the year. He found those of Baines to be the most accurate. He undertook many long treks up river, and visited Paramount Chief Lewanika of the Barotse. On a return visit to Britain in about 1905 he gave a number of lantern lectures in London and elsewhere, entitled "A Thousand Miles in a Dug-out", illustrated with his own photographs. This must rate him as one of the earliest of Rhodesia's publicists.

His travel and photographic work brought recognition in his election as a Fellow of the Royal Geographical Society; a Fellow of the Royal Colonial Institute; and in 1925, the year in which the Prince of Wales visited the Falls, as an Associate of the Royal Photographic Society. Meantime his quaint shop, 'The Huts', had become world renowned. Tens of thousands of visitors passed through its humble thatched portals, among them many notables, even royalty. With a keen eye to business, he imported nine canoes from Canada and a motor launch from Durban in 1908, and for a while operated a ricksha service. He was the originator of the idea of the trolley line from the hotel to the bridge.

When Mr. Leo Weinthal started publishing *The African World*, Mr. Clark was appointed correspondent at the Victoria Falls. Further appointments followed, among them Reuters, The Exchange Telegraph Company, London, *The Cambridge Chronicle*, and several South African papers.

Percy Clark who lived at the Victoria Falls until his death in 1937 has left a rich pictorial and written record of life on the Zambesi. He was one of the most colourful of the early settlers, a 'character' with a ready wit and sense of humour whose reminiscences and anecdotes give a fascinating picture of the rough but romantic days when this part of Africa passed from savagery to civilisation.

We wish to acknowledge the co-operation received from Mr. Victor Clark in the production of this reprint, and from the original publishers, George G. Harrap & Co. Ltd. of London, who kindly permitted its reproduction in facsimile.

L.W.B.

Bulawayo,
December 1972.
©

THE AUTOBIOGRAPHY OF
AN OLD DRIFTER

THE AUTHOR

Photo Jocelyn Leigh-Hunt, Durban

Fr.

The Autobiography of
An Old Drifter

THE LIFE-STORY OF
Percy M. Clark
OF VICTORIA FALLS

WITH A FOREWORD BY
SIR HERBERT J. STANLEY G.C.M.G.
Governor of Southern Rhodesia

AND THIRTY-TWO ILLUSTRATIONS FROM
PHOTOGRAPHS

GEORGE G. HARRAP & CO. LTD.
LONDON   BOMBAY   SYDNEY

First published 1936
by George G. Harrap & Co. Ltd.
182 *High Holborn, London,* W.C.1

*Made in Great Britain. Printed by Sherratt & Hughes,
at the St Ann's Press, Manchester*

FOREWORD

AMONG the thousands of visitors to the Victoria Falls there are but few who fail to find their way to the picturesque huts built and occupied by Mr Percy Clark, and to acquire there, from his stock of curios, mainly of native craftsmanship, or from his varied assortment of photographs and postcards, some memento for themselves or some gift for absent friends. And I venture to think that to very many of such visitors any conversation which they may have had with the owner of the huts will have proved the most interesting item of their acquisitions. For Mr Clark is not only a survivor from the brave bygone days of the very early settlers, but is also a ' character,' generous in drawing upon a seemingly inexhaustible fund of reminiscence and anecdote and in seasoning his output with a ready wit and a sense of humour, usually genial, occasionally pungent.

I have known Mr Clark, off and on, for the last quarter of a century, and have had many a good talk with him. Often I have wished that there might be some permanent record of his adventures in Rhodesia and of the impact of conditions, long since superseded, upon a mind then youthful as well as receptive. In the memory of men such as he there lies embedded much of the unwritten history, much of the romance, of the European penetration into Central Africa—a chequered tale in some respects, but also a tale of unflinching courage, indomitable endurance, and a copious measure of human kindness. I was glad, therefore, when Mr Clark told me, a month or two ago, that he had written his memoirs, and very gladly I agreed to contribute to them a few words by way of preface.

I have now read the book in typescript. It is characteristic of its author—vivid, unsophisticated, candid in substance and in diction. There is in it little that is not likely to be of interest even to readers to whom Rhodesia is but a name. It is marked by a commendable absence of dull or sententious passages. My only quarrel with it is in regard to some of its references to the native population. Although in the days which preceded the establishment of ordered conditions rough-and-ready methods may well have been unavoidable, both Mr Clark personally and Rhodesians generally have kindly feelings towards their native employees, and maintain with them relations devoid neither of sympathy nor of understanding.

Having said this, I need only add that, in my judgment, Mr Clark's account of his experiences as one of the 'old hands' in Southern Rhodesia and in the Zambesi Valley of Northern Rhodesia throws an illuminating sidelight on more conventional records, and I have no doubt that a large number of readers will find something to learn, and much to entertain them, in the sprightly pages of his narrative.

H. J. STANLEY

GOVERNMENT HOUSE
SALISBURY
SOUTHERN RHODESIA

CONTENTS

CHAPTER   PAGE

I. EARLY YEARS IN CAMBRIDGE   11

II. GROWING UP   27

III. I FIND MY OCCUPATION   38

IV. SOUTHWARD HO!   43

V. ROUGH DOINGS   61

VI. CONTACTS WITH CECIL RHODES   77

VII. ON TREK   89

VIII. OFF AGAIN   103

IX. FIRST SAFARI   116

X. UP THE ZAMBESI   131

XI. UP-RIVER AND DOWN AGAIN   144

XII. DIVERS TROUBLES   160

XIII. THE OLD DRIFT   175

XIV. THE GORGE OF THE FALLS   188

XV. THE RAILWAY COMES   202

XVI. HOME FOR A WIFE   214

XVII. MY WIFE AND I   227

XVIII. UPS AND DOWNS   243

XIX. WE CARRY ON   260

ILLUSTRATIONS

PAGE

THE AUTHOR · · · · · · · · *Frontispiece*

A DUST-DEVIL AT BULAWAYO · · · · · 50

HANGING SPIES IN THE MAIN STREET OF BULAWAYO
DURING THE MATABELE REBELLION, 1896 · · 66

A SWIMMING-POOL NEAR BULAWAYO · · · · 74

CECIL RHODES BY THE SITE OF HIS GRAVE IN THE
MATOPPOS · · · · · · · · · 80

CROSSING THE BLANKET DRIFT WITH A DOUBLE SPAN
OF THIRTY-TWO OXEN · · · · · · 92

A FLASHLIGHT PHOTOGRAPH TAKEN IN THE GEELONG
MINE · · · · · · · · · · 100

THE AUTHOR AND O'CONNOR BEFORE LEAVING FOR THE
ZAMBESI · · · · · · · · · 108

SABLE ANTELOPE SHOT ON THE ROAD TO WANKIE · 112

MY CARRIERS · · · · · · · · · 116

WATER-HOLES IN THE VELDT · · · · · 120

BAOBAB-TREE NEAR THE FALLS · · · · · 124

THE CHASM FROM THE WESTERN END OF THE FALLS · 128

MY PROSPECTOR FRIENDS · · · · · · 134

BEATING TOM-TOMS OUTSIDE LITIA'S PALACE · · 138

LITIA · · · · · · · · · · 142

DUG-OUTS ON THE WAY TO LIA-LUI · · · 146

PORTAGE AT N'GONYE FALLS · · · · · 150

THE NELA KWANDA · · · · · · · 154

MY FLEET OF DUG-OUTS · · · · · · 158

FISHING WITH ASSEGAIS · · · · · · 162

NATIVE BLACKSMITHS · · · · · · · 166

9

	PAGE
MY SLEEPING-SHELTER	170
REED BUCK SHOT BY THE AUTHOR	172
ON THE BANKS OF THE ZAMBESI	176
FOX CROSSING THE GORGE	192
THE BRIDGE DURING CONSTRUCTION	196
THE BRIDGE COMPLETED	202
THE MAIN FALL	210
LEOPARD SHOT AT THE HUTS	234
SIR HERBERT STANLEY AND SIR CECIL RODWELL FISHING ON THE ZAMBESI	252
THE OLD-TIMER	268

CHAPTER I

EARLY YEARS IN CAMBRIDGE

I WAS born in Cambridge at ten o'clock on New Year's Eve in the year 1874. If I had been born two hours later it would have been in the year 1875, and it has always seemed to me that I'd have been a year younger. Whether the difference of two hours is a matter for regret or not is a thing about which I haven't yet made up my mind. I have been told that the night of my birth was an exceptionally cold and frosty one, with ice in the streets and pedestrians slipping all over them. I can't remember, however, that I took any great interest in weather conditions at the time.

I was one of a family of ten: eight boys and two girls. I achieved the reputation of being the rudest of the family. The justice of this I stoutly deny, though I do admit that usually I had the blame for any mischief that was done.

My father had been first mate of a sailing-ship before he married. He was short in stature and had curly hair, I remember, and he was quite the gentleman. His shortness and his gentility were nevertheless no hindrance on one occasion, when a great hefty navvy walked off with something of mine. My father caught the man, who showed fight. The fellow may have imagined he had picked an easy one, but Dad made rings round him.

My mother was of the gentler kind, and, my father dying before the last of the family was born, she was hard put to it to keep things going for her large brood. One or other of us was able to go to the Grammar School, but the rest of us, myself among them, had to be content with an ordinary day school. But this, as far as I was concerned, came later in my boyhood.

Actually my first schooling was at an ' academy ' run by an old dame, the fees being about twopence a week. I would be five or thereabout when I was sent there, the idea being, I suppose, to keep me out of mischief. I cannot imagine that I learned much in this first essay. It was a phase, at all events, that came to an abrupt end. The children, entering the school yard one morning, came upon an old-fashioned wash-tub full of blood and water. The old dame had cut her throat. Looking after us imps had been too much for her, I suppose.

The next school I attended was also a ' dame's school,' but a bigger one. The old lady who ran it held a mixed class in the afternoons, she on a dais and the scholars in a circle below. She had a habit of dropping off into a half-hour's snooze each day. When this happened her pupils became busy in chewing paper to a pulp. Out of this pulp nice soft balls could be made, and these could be projected by the aid of a piece of steel spring. Projected, they landed with a nice squelchy smack. The old lady was the target for the more daring, and a hit on her nose was considered a bull's-eye. There were, of course, more inners and outers than bull's-eyes, and once in a way the old dame got an earful. When this occurred the old lady would heave herself from her chair, pick up a cane, and give the chief offenders a couple of good 'uns. Then, having prophesied a little on our ultimate fates, she would return to her chair and slumber.

Once the old lady asked all her pupils to tea in the garden. It was a good party in its way, and we made the most of it. But it happened that the garden contained a water-butt full to the brim. Naturally the boys made the most of this discovery, and the bulk of us were soaked in no time. Then the spigot came out. We did our best to stem the flood with hands and handkerchiefs, but the end was a complete drenching for those not already soaked, and the garden looking like a miniature pond. That finished the garden party. We were sent home, and there were no more of these *fêtes* while I was at the school. Many years later I heard that our old school-marm died in a lunatic asylum. The emotions evoked by the intelligence did not include that of surprise.

My education was carried on in still another dame's school, even more select than the last. It was also co-educational, the female pupils being instructed by a Miss Copping and the boys by a Miss Williams, familiarly spoken of as ' Sally.' The school curriculum was made up of the three R's, with music and singing. Sally instructed in pianoforte. I was a piano pupil. What I remember best about Sally's methods was the pencil she used to suck most of the time. When she wasn't sucking it she used it for rapping knuckles to indicate mistakes. This knuckle-rapping, with the imposition of penalties for misdemeanours, was Sally's main occupation—" a dozen sums, Master Clark," or, " a dozen sums, Master Howes." Poor Tom Howes was always in a burdened state. He often had as many as six dozen in hand.

I remember that some Latin was taught, mainly

because of my impression that each lesson was mugged up by the teacher just beforehand. The word *niger* turned up in one morning lesson. The mistress was asked the proper pronunciation. She was in some doubt on the matter, and the ruling was deferred until the afternoon. Then the decision was solemnly announced in class. " We have decided," it ran, " that the proper pronunciation shall be ' niger,' not ' nigger.' "

At the age of nine I was a chorister at the oldest of the Cambridge colleges, St Peter's. The familiar name for it was ' Peterhouse,' but some of us, of course, made it ' Pothouse.' Of this particular phase in my young existence I have the most happy memories. Young as I was, I thought the old College beautiful, with its ancient walls feet thick. There was a small park attached to it which had deer, and beyond this was the Fellows' garden. Here, after chapel on Sunday mornings, I passed many a lovely hour, lying on the velvety turf reading or watching the birds. These were many in number and variety, for the garden was a real sanctuary to them.

We choristers had to assemble before chapel in the Combination-room to put on our surplices. When the Dean arrived we had to march in stately procession through the Old Court to the Chapel itself. I remember the Chapel best for its lovely stained windows, and for the absolute peace that pervaded the Sanctuary. Often after the service we choir-boys would sit and listen to the fine old organ played by a master. This was William Amps, and dear old fellow he was, too.

Not long after I joined the choir the College celebrated its six-hundredth anniversary, and with the rest

I sang before the Duke of Clarence, who took part in the celebrations. My most vivid recollection of the occasion is a boyish one—the magnificent tuck-in which was given the choristers, and which, you may be sure, we boys waded into in good style.

It may be imagined—choir-boys being what they are —that we young rascals did not always keep the saintly demeanour we exhibited in chapel itself. There were great larks in the Combination-room before service began, and booby-traps for the late-comers were our pet diversions. The Dean, a particularly gentle-mannered and inoffensive soul, happened to turn up a trifle earlier than usual one morning, and walked right into one of our most elaborate contraptions of this kind. It was funny to see his look of mild surprise as he emerged from the shower of books, dustpans, brooms, and other oddments that descended as he pushed open the door. But his rebuke was a classic for mildness. " Boys! Boys! " he said. " You shouldn't do that, you know! "

Another of our amusements had to do with the tallow candles with which, in all sizes, the Chapel was lit. Those near the altar were enormous. After the service was over there was competition among us in blowing out the candles and collecting the grease that, especially in a draught, would run down them in great streaks. The grease could be moulded into all sorts of shapes, but this was not the least messy of the uses we found for it.

Ultimately, of course, my voice broke, but for two years before that happened I was one of the two soloists in the choir.

Yes, indeed. The happiest days of my early life belonged to this phase of it.

As a youngster I always had pets. Our house was an old one, inhabited from the building of it by the Clark family. It had eleven rooms, and in the yard at the back were sheds with lofts, to which one ascended by a ladder. These buildings were ideal for playing in, and the loft a fine place for housing pets. Rabbits were accommodated in the loft, but the white rats—of which I had twenty or more—I would insist in keeping in my bedroom.

This habit, it may be guessed, caused great delight among the older members of my family. The old buck rat was an enormous chap, with hair like wire. At night, somehow or other, he would get out of his cage and into my bed to settle by my side. Once when I was down with influenza our family doctor arrived, to find the whole score of my white rats on my bed. He was of the sort to be tickled rather than shocked by the spectacle, and his name for me thereafter was ' White Rat.'

I had a succession of jackdaws for pets about this time, and they were all very amusing companions. There was one in particular who was my great friend, a faithful follower wherever I went. " Up, Jack! " would bring him flying to my shoulder. I took him with me all over the town, and everybody knew ' Clark's jackdaw.' But he was an artful beggar, whose predatory habits made it unsafe to leave any bright object lying about. I once wandered with him into a plantation where some boys were playing marbles. They were playing that variety of the game—I forget its name—where the idea is to get the marbles into three holes in a line. I fell to watching the game, leaving Jack to wander about on his own. There was a glass ' alley ' among the marbles. If the commandment about coveting can be broken by a bird, it was never so badly smashed as when Jack saw that alley.

Though I now remember Jack's manœuvres, I don't believe at the time that I realized what they meant. The artfulness of the little devil! To have seen him strutting around you'd have thought the last thing he had his mind on was that coloured bit of glass. He never as much as looked at it. The farthest hole from the shooting-base, so to call it, was close to a tree, and the alley was in the hole. But the boys were close to the hole. Jack had his back to the marble, and was amusing himself, apparently, with pecking at the tree. You may be sure, all the same, that there was a backward cock in his weather eye, because the moment the boys moved away he was round in a flash. And where was that alley? Ask of the winds that far around . . . There was racing and chasing. . . .

Jack lived in the back premises, and I spent hours with him teaching him to talk. He had the run of the cart-shed and the loft. When I got home from school my first thought was to call Jack, and he always answered.

There came a Sunday morning when I got back from church and called him. There was no answer. I called again and again, then went in search. I found him at last in a corner of the cart-shed. He was stone-dead. What actually killed him I never found out—he probably had picked up something poisoned; even now I can feel something of the boyish pang I experienced in losing my good pal.

I was always pretty good with birds as a boy, and I tamed several to the point of getting them to perch on my fingers and feed from my lips. But I remember my disappointment at being able to make so little out of a hedgehog. He never was at all responsive, and all he did for me was get me into trouble with the rest of my family by his annoying way of turning up in all sorts of unexpected places.

There was a tortoise, too, that I tried hard to make a pet of, but he was as self-centred as the hedgehog. I never got a blink of recognition out of him. Still, there was one prank in which he played principal part, and which justified his existence in boyish eyes.

We had a parson staying with us, the Rev. Henry John. It was a cold winter. One night, just before the Rev. H. J. retired to bed, I slipped into his room and shoved the tortoise well down between the sheets. As soon as H. J. got into his room my brothers and myself collected outside his door to listen. Presently, to our extreme delight, a series of shrieks came from the room. We rushed in. There was his reverence in his night-gown jumping up and down and scared almost stiff. He explained that when he got into bed his feet had met with a cold moving object. (What could be colder or more loathsome of movement in a bed than a tortoise?) Of course, we investigated the matter sympathetically, and wondered how on earth the tortoise could have got there; but I cannot imagine that the Rev. Henry was deceived by our play-acting.

He wasn't a bad sort, the Rev. H. J. I was seated next to him one evening at supper. I was, you may remember, the bad boy of the family. The cold joint was in process of being carved. To my left was a cold rice pudding, with a creamy sort of custard top, and by it was a tablespoon. A big fly lighted on the pudding. Without a second's contemplation of cause and effect, I picked up the spoon. " This is Dick Whittaker and a blow-fly! " says I, and brought the spoon down smack on the fly. But I also brought it smack down on the pudding, splattering the eggy layer all over the place. The feat of killing the fly didn't go down well with the family. But the Rev. H. J., after a second or two of struggle to keep a solemn face, put his hands on the table and fairly howled with laughter. I simply couldn't see why that pudding should have been removed. The fly didn't hurt it.

The Dick Whittaker I thought I was impersonating was our butcher. He was a great swell on Sundays in his frock-coat and top-hat. One Sunday, when he was getting his topper out of its case in preparation for going to church he found a snake in it. Dick yelled and streaked for the door. He never discovered how the snake got into his topper, but, oddly enough, my brother lost a grass-snake that very Sunday.

Whittaker had a son and a slaughter-house, and the one used to organize rat-hunts in the other. The place was infested with rats, so that the hunting normally was good. We armed ourselves with knives and sticks, and Dick junior had an old sword. There was a ledge that the rats would run along, and there young Dick smote them hip and thigh, so that, with our help, the slaughter was often appropriate to the hunting-ground. A blood-thirsty generation we must have been then, because we found great interest in the pole-axing and cutting up of the bullocks there, and in the sheep having their throats cut, or the pigs that went squealing to their deaths. Another interest in the slaughter-house for us was in the maggots for fishing that we could get there. Fine fat maggots they were, and excellent bait. One good piece of offal left for a day or two provided us with all the maggots we could possibly want.

We spent a lot of time on the river then, canoeing, swimming, and fishing. There was a Canadian canoe that we could hire for sixpence an hour, the lightest on the river. With ourselves in the stern and its bows cocked up, it could be turned on the space of half a crown. In this cockleshell we would paddle up-river to Granchester mill. Here we would bathe, but our great delight was to paddle right up to the mill and shoot the mill-race. It was great sport, in which we were often upset, but we were good swimmers and thought capsiz-ing part of the fun. I didn't know it then, but in later years I was to shoot miles of rapids on a mightier river by far, the Zambesi, in native dug-outs. I wonder just how much those early pranks had to do with my later taste for adventure. In those early days I spent many a night fishing for eels, and most often in the summer I was up and astir by four o'clock in the morning.

One event of my boyhood in Cambridge which had distinct influence on my later life was the presentation to me, at the age of twelve, of a camera with all the necessary paraphernalia: ruby lamp, developing dishes, plates, and so forth. It was a complete boy-photographer's set at half a guinea. The camera was simply a box with an old spectacle glass for lens, fixed into place with a piece of brass wire. The lens was focused by pulling it in and out. Of course, I took photographs of my friends and relations. As I usually posed them in a room with their backs to the window, the results were weird to a degree. I gave my sitters prints, but retained copies for myself. These, later on, I stuck in an album. This I called my book of " 'a-penny 'orribles and penny dreadfuls." I haven't named anything more aptly since.

Some time later I came into possession of a half-plate camera, and with this I did some fairly good work. It is so long ago that I can say that without the feeling of bragging. But for my first camera I made myself a darkroom under the stairs, in a cupboard. With the lantern burning, the place became extremely hot, and I sweated as copiously while developing plates as if I had been in a Turkish bath. I was at a good deal of pains to make the cupboard light-proof. For a couple of days I plastered up all the cracks with ruby canvas, with gratifying results. True, I excluded all air, but I also excluded all raw light. Then, after all my labours, within the next week the cupboard was cleaned and scrubbed during spring-cleaning. The red canvas was scrubbed off the walls, and I had to begin all over again.

With mention of my photographic activities, however, I get too far ahead with my story. I have to get back to my schooling.

At the age of nine I was sent to a large school for boys, where I began in the fourth standard. By the time I was fifteen I was head of the school, in spite of the fact that my reports usually bore a footnote: " Plenty of ability, but no application." For the first year I did try to be a good boy, and succeeded to the extent of never being haled before the Head to get the stick. But my first caning chanced to be inflicted on me without just cause, and after that I felt I didn't care a damn. With the smirching of my hard-won reputation the incentive to careful behaviour was gone. I had an obstinate nature. I could have been led to Hell, but not driven to Heaven. The business of the physiology class is a case in point.

Science classes in that school were held during midday recess—that is, from twelve to one o'clock. As we had to be back in school by two-fifteen, these classes docked a considerable portion of the time allotted for food and recreation. Physiology was one of the subjects dealt with, but, while compulsory for the class above that which I was in, it was optional for mine. The master lecturing on this subject asked me if I would care to join. Since I had an option in the matter, I said, " No, thanks. It is not in my line." " Well," returned the master, " come to the first lecture, and if you don't like it you needn't go on." That sounded fair enough, and I went.

When the lecture day came round in the following week I informed the master that I preferred to be absent. He said, however, that as my name was down on the list I had lost the option, and that I would have to attend. Of course I protested. My protestations were useless. " All right," said I. " If I've got to attend, I've got to—but I won't take any notes, and I will fail in the examination." Next week the notes on the previous

22

lecture were examined, but there was none from me. I was haled before the Head for correction. The process of inactivity and correction went on right to the end of the session. I was made to attend the examination, but handed in a blank paper.

Next year the lecture was compulsory for me, and, just to show them, I passed first-class. The year after that I got a second-class in the advanced stage—just to show them.

There was one enthusiastic lecturer on another science subject whose expositions ran on to one-thirty. We were supposed to be set free at one o'clock. That extra half-hour left us little time for getting home, having a decent meal, and returning at the usual hour. A protest meeting was held one day after class, and a resolution was passed. We were to meet, all of us, on Parker's Piece—a large playground—and go in procession to school, arriving at three. Just before three I turned up at Parker's Piece. I found myself alone, and I had to do the procession all by myself. I reached school at three to find that the others had got there at the usual time. Explanation of my unpunctuality was demanded by the Head, and I told him all. It did not save me from the usual caning. Still, my martyrdom was of some effect, for things were better from the scholars' point of view from then on.

When eventually my schooldays were over I had the luck to get a job with Mr J. West Knights, Public Analyst for Cambridge. I conceived a liking for my first boss straight away. He was a fine old chap, sporting a black beard. When he was considering some problem, he had a trick of cocking his head sideways and up, and scratching through the side of this chin fungus.

Mr Knights fixed up a laboratory for me in a room over his own. And here, by dint of much experiment on my own, and from instruction from my boss, I learned quite a lot of chemistry. After a time I was allowed to make analyses of water, milk, and marl. Then there were artificial manures. These were particularly interesting, both as regards composition and odour. But there was no end to the odd materials that came our way for examination: poisoned beasts, the crops of birds, human stomachs—a strangely varied collection indeed. Not least curious of the substances that came to us for analysis were the samples of milk and water brought in by the sanitary inspectors. It is not to be imagined what unhealthy things we found in them. Nor were the human contacts involved in the work less interesting than the work itself. I remember in particular the Sanitary Inspector for the suburban districts. He was a fine fellow, but amusingly ' countryfied ' in his brogue and phrases. Outside his own particular sphere he waged great war on the " wopses and wums " that, as he put it, " mucked up " his fruit and vegetables.

My boss was exceedingly kind-hearted, with a great sense of humour. He had a quiet habit of leg-pulling. He told me once, when I was wrapping up a disinfecting pump arrangement: " Always tie the label on with double knots; it shows the stuff comes from a good firm." I was trusting enough, or callow enough, to believe him. But, for me, the great thing about Mr Knights was his understanding of boyish longings. On days when bright sunshine made a lad ache for the open air he would invariably let me go at three-thirty or four o'clock. If I asked for a holiday, he never refused. He would scratch his beard reflectively and murmur, " We-e-ll— I don't think I shall want you this afternoon." And as soon as twelve noon arrived he would say, " You can run along now."

I remember going to him with the query: " Mr Knights, I have an invitation to go to Switzerland for a three weeks' walking-tour—may I accept it? " In his usual way he cocked his head sideways and scratched his beard. " Yes, Percy," he said, after cogitating for a moment or two. " I don't think I shall want you." That, of course, was not too complimentary, but perhaps it indicates what sort of man my first boss was.

In connexion with my holiday in Switzerland there was an odd episode. In preparation for the climbing, and so on, that I expected to have I took a pair of boots to the shoemaker's to have stout nails put in the soles. On my way back home from the cobbler's I found I had lost one of the boots. After searching for it vainly I went to the police-station and reported the loss. A notice was put up offering a reward of half a crown for the missing boot. As the station sergeant remarked, " A single boot was no good to anybody." Still, the boot was not brought in before the day of my departure, and I went to Switzerland without it.

On my return home a note awaited me saying the boot had been recovered. It had been found by a country carrier who came into town to market on one day only each week. That happened to be the day in the week when I dropped the boot. The carrier had only one leg, and my boot fitted his solitary foot perfectly.

I got back to Cambridge three days later than I should have done, and on the morning after my arrival I went round to Mr Knights' house to get the laboratory keys. There was no reply to my knocks and rings. Mr Knights had gone off for a month's holiday on his own account, so that I had a holiday of seven weeks altogether in glorious summer weather.

It all may sound as if my boss was rather too casual, but he did, in fact, give me a good training. To supplement this, I studied in the evenings. I had, moreover, a lot of coaching from some of the University lecturers, men who offered free tuition to a few who were keen on their work. This tuition included practical instruction in the lecturers' own laboratories in qualitative and quantitative analysis and in organic and inorganic chemistry. Among those who coached us in the winter months was Colonel Haycock.

CHAPTER II

GROWING UP

AFTER about three years with Mr Knights, the Public Analyst, I was offered a place as assistant at the University laboratories. For three or four years there I worked under the late Professor Liveing and Dr Easterfield. As Professor Liveing's assistant it was my duty to prepare all experiments for his lectures, and to carry them out while he lectured. He often cursed me plenty, but he would not let anyone else do this work for him.

Professor Liveing was inclined to be peppery. It happened once while he was lecturing that the students paid more attention to the illustrative experiment I was going through than to what the Professor was saying about it. "Attend to me!" the old man snapped. "Any fool could do that experiment."

The students had a way, after the lectures were over, of crowding round the lecture bench to examine the apparatus and ask questions. On this particular day the usual crowd came round, and quite a number clustered about me. As I was giving some explanation one of the students broke in: "Oh, any fool could do that." "Yes," I replied quietly, "you could do it perfectly." That switched the guffaws to the interrupter, and he faded away.

I was often with Professor Liveing when he was doing research work, and it happened on one of those occasions that he simply could not arrive at the main idea. The trouble was, perhaps, that the old man was thinking along complicated lines, while the explanation he sought was essentially simple. I suggested the simple explanation. He went clean off the deep end over my impertinence, as he thought it, and began to run up and down the laboratory stairs in a rage. " What do you know of chemistry? " he fumed. " You, a mere infant, presume to teach me, with my seventy years' experience! " And so on, and so on. But after a while he cooled down and accepted my suggestion. The thing was too simple for the immensity of his mind—but " any fool " could have seen it.

Professor Liveing was a real character. He was the oldest and the senior Professor in Cambridge. He always wore a grey flannel shirt with no tie. Royalty on one occasion came to visit the city, and as senior professor the old man had to meet them. The only concession in costume for this great event that he made was to stick in his collar a huge cornelian stud about the size of half a crown. At the age of ninety-nine, while walking to his work at the laboratory, he was knocked over by a cyclist. The shock was too much for him and he died a few months later. But he worked up to the last, and his death was a real loss to science. I count it a great privilege to have worked for him.

During the time that I was working at the University laboratories, Professor (afterwards Sir John) Dewar liquified air; his first lecture was a great demonstration. It was he who discovered cordite, the smokeless powder. It was during this time, too, that the X-rays were discovered. A fellow assistant and myself constructed a home-made apparatus, he doing most of the glass-blowing, and with it we took a skiagraph of a girl's hand with a ring on one of her fingers. The experiment was entirely successful, the photograph showing the bones of the hand and the ring on the finger. I can, therefore, claim to be among the first to take an X-ray photograph in England.

I need hardly say, of course, that I was not long a working chemist before I had fixed up a laboratory of my own at home. This was just about as popular with my family as my hedgehog had been, or my white rats. And it may be imagined that, among my early experiments, sulphuretted hydrogen did not fail to be included in my manufactures. I leave it to you to imagine how heads were poked out of windows around my home lab., and what remarks were fired at me from all sides on such occasions.

I can honestly say for myself that I did work hard in the years I was employed at the University laboratories. I had to be on the job at nine in the mornings, and I did not get away until six in the afternoon. In the evenings, as I have said, I studied. For three years I was coached in natural science by a Fellow of Trinity. This was a brilliant scholar who took a double first in the Tripos, becoming a Fellow of Trinity at the age of twenty-three —the youngest Fellow on record. He coached me for a scholarship at one of the colleges, and he said himself that I had every chance of winning it. But, unfortunately, the very year I entered for this scholarship it was withdrawn. I was over age for most other scholarships in my own line, and in my disappointment and disgust I gave up chemistry altogether.

Other circumstances combined to dishearten me. I was in an odd position. I knew enough, my tutor said, to pass a Tripos, but I lacked, or had forgotten, the preliminary education to get through the Little-go, that examination which enables one to matriculate at the University. I had, however, been having some coaching for the Little-go, but could not afford to enter unless I was working at the same time. I went to the Professor, my boss, and asked to be allowed to study for my degrees while still working in the laboratories. He would not permit it, and his refusal was another thing that made me chuck the whole bag of tricks.

Then, again, I had worked myself sick. My state of health was brought home to me by an unpleasant experience. I had been to the May races with my brother. On the way home we fell in with a couple of friends in the principal street of the town, and we stopped to have a chat outside the door of one of them, a chemist. In the middle of our chat I said suddenly, half in fun : " I say, you chaps, I am going to faint." They chaffed me, called me a silly ass, and said I couldn't faint if I tried. But I must have done just that, because the next thing I knew was that I was in my friend's house, with him and his mother bending over me anxiously. The doctor who was called in diagnosed overwork, and I had to give up study for a time and take a holiday.

Having worked to the extent of making myself ill, I was in no mood to put up with those several disappointments and hindrances in my proposed career as a chemist. It all seemed hopeless, and I took another kind of job altogether. It will be seen later how this led to a complete change in my life. But I must not digress ; there are some other interests of my youthful days that I will first deal with.

In my adolescence I found great interest in thought transmission—what is sometimes called mental telepathy. My first essays were at Christmas parties, where it was the subject of a game. But it happened that I was rather good as a medium, and I pursued the idea more seriously than most. With some people I was curiously successful. I had a friend, a great chum, called Billy Hook. Billy left Cambridge and went to live at Bristol. Before we parted we arranged to try to get *en rapport* at a certain hour each night. The experiment never had any real success.

One evening, however, as I was coming home from the laboratory, I became aware that Billy Hook was in the town. When I got home I asked my mother straight away: " Where's Billy Hook? " " In Bristol, isn't he? " she replied. " No," said I, " he's in this house." My mother said I was talking nonsense, I knew Billy was in Bristol. " No, Mother—he's here," I insisted. " Ah! " said my mother. " You saw his hat hung up in the hall, I suppose? " " No, I didn't," I said quite truthfully, " but I know he's here in this house." And Billy was. He had come on a surprise visit.

My only other great chum at this time was Percy French, who later married my sister. We did some quite remarkable things in telepathy. I was blindfolded and, with my temples lightly held, was willed to do certain things, even to the writing of words. Our success with this method was invariable.

Some years after this, while I was manager of a

photographic studio in Norwich, I told my landlady at breakfast one morning that I expected a friend to call. I had received no material communication, believe me, to justify the expectation. But so certain was I that Percy French was coming that I told my landlady to send him up to the studio when he arrived. Noon came, and there was no Percy. I got back to my digs at five-thirty, still so convinced that Percy was coming that I waited tea for him for over an hour. Then, instead of going as usual to the club that night, I remained at home. But nothing happened. Next day I wrote to Percy French and told him of how I had felt and of what I had done. When his answer came I learned that he had actually passed through Norwich that morning on his way to Yarmouth, where he had some business to transact, and that he had returned through Norwich that night. He had not, *as he had hoped*, had time to call on me.

Once about this period I had a curious experience in Yarmouth. The Yarmouth races were on, and with a friend I went to the meeting. Neither of us had any continuing interest in horse-racing, nor did we know the name of a single horse at this meeting. When we arrived at the course we bought a race-card. There were six races. My friend said that we ought to have a bob or two on the first race. "What shall we back?" he said. I looked at the list of runners, and it seemed to me that the name of one horse stuck out bolder than the others, in big black letters. We put half a crown apiece on this horse. It won. Well, not to pad out the story, the same thing happened in the next four races. I saw a horse's name bolder than the rest, we backed it, and it won in each instance.

When it came to the last race I could see nothing. My friend, flushed with success, said: " Well, I'm going to back something." "All right," I replied, "put your money on with me, and if the horse wins I'll give you the starting price." He did this. The horse he picked lost, so I won on all six races.

There was a sequel to this. It happened twenty-eight years later, but it will not be out of place to tell of it now. In Africa I was on my way to the coast for a holiday, and I happened to drop into the Bulawayo Club, where I fell in with two friends. After the usual greetings and so on, I was asked: " Well, P.M., what's going to win the Cambridgeshire?" "Ask me another," I returned. " I don't back horses, and I don't know the name of a single runner." Then I related my experience at Yarmouth races twenty-eight years previously. The story set my two friends agog, and one of them handed me a list of the Cambridgeshire runners. " Have a look at this," he said, " and see what you can do." I protested that the Yarmouth affair had happened a long time before, and that it wasn't at all likely such clairvoyance would occur again. I was urged to try, anyhow, and I did. It was no good, as I quite expected. The more eager of the two handed me a list of runners in the Metropolitan, a race run in the Cape Province, and he urged me to try with that. There were about seventy entries. I concentrated on this, and it did seem as if one horse stood out above the others. " Yes," I said, " I can see a horse." Of course they wanted to know which one. " I am not telling you," said I. " You might back it and lose." But at the same time I fixed the horse's name in my mind. It was suggested then that I should have

C 33

another look, and this I did. A second name stood out and I told my friends what it was. The experiment was made again, and a third name was noted.

That same day I left for Durban. The race was run a month later. The horse whose name I had first seen standing out was the winner, and the other two were second and third in the order of appearance. I still have a letter from one of the friends in the Bulawayo Club confirming these facts.

One of the major pleasures of my youthful days in Cambridge was walking. My particular chum, Percy French, and myself often covered twenty to thirty miles on Sundays. A favourite walk of ours on a Sunday afternoon was to Haslingfield, a little village about eight miles from Cambridge. The ramble was by fields and country lanes, through the Granchester meadows, by farm paths and by streams, and never for any distance by made roads. On our arrival at the village inn, where we were well known, we would have tea—and what a tea! Home-made bread, home-churned butter, new-laid eggs, watercress, lettuce, radishes, celery, and fruit according to the season. We could go into the garden and pick greengages, apples, and so forth to eat to our heart's content. The charge for all this was ninepence!

On these rambles the idea that we might be trespassing never exercised the minds of Percy and myself. As a fact, prohibitory notices and the idea of man-traps added zest to our venturing. Once when we had followed a brook and climbed an iron railing which obviously enclosed private property—our objective being a road a mile or so ahead—we encountered the owner of the land when we were half-way. He had a shot-gun under his arm and two or three dogs at his heels. He pounced on us. " What are you doing on my land?" he shouted. " Don't you know you're trespassing?"

" Yes, of course we know," was our reply. " But what about it? We are doing no harm."

" Get off the place!" he yelled. " I'll set the dogs on you! I'll prosecute you!"

" Prosecute?" we echoed cheekily. " Well—you'll have to prove damage before you can get damages."

" You young devils!" he exclaimed. " Get off my land quick, or I'll give you a damned good hiding!"

That was talking. We knew he meant that. And off we cleared.

The England of to-day seems, from a distance, a tamer and less spacious England than that of my youth. In the years during which I worked at the University laboratories, and before I left Cambridge, there always seemed to be fun going on in the town. Rags were plentiful and varied. There were the November Fifth scraps in which Town opposed Gown, with on Market Hill a big bonfire, which was kept ablaze by fuel obtained in raids far afield. Hoardings were pulled down and broken up, shutters, goal-posts from afar, anything was seized that would burn. I remember once seeing a barrel put over the head of a policeman, and that individual shoved towards the fire. Fortunately, humaner instincts prevailed before he reached it. In those rags the helmet of a policeman was considered a great trophy, and it was just as well that the Cambridge police were a set of good-natured officers. They took the rags in good part, and were not a bit averse from scrapping. It was when the County police were called in to take a hand—in my idea a great mistake—that things took a serious turn. Proctors and their bulldogs were kept busy.

The biggest rag I ever saw was when Kitchener came to Cambridge, after the Sudan War, to be given an honorary degree. The press was so heavy that the Senate House railings fell down. The Sirdar's sister was the wife of the Master of Christ's College, and Kitchener stayed there. As he left the Senate House the horses were taken out of his carriage, and it was pulled and pushed to Christ's. The carriage was hauled through the large double gates, and about fifty of us got into the quad with it before the porters managed to close the gates.

Those inside would not allow Kitchener to retire until he had made a speech. To this day I remember his steel-grey eyes, on that occasion with a twinkle in them, and I remember his speech. It was short and to the point. " Boys," he said, " I had a hot time in the Sudan, but I've had a damned sight hotter time to-day. I only wish that I'd had you there with me. Good morning! "

That night was the wildest in my experience of Cambridge. The pavilions from the College football grounds, palings, and the wooden fence about the University buildings and schools were uplifted and dragged to make fuel for a bonfire. In the unshipping of one fence a lamp-post was wrecked, and the gas issuing from the pipe was set alight. It made a tremendous flare. The fire brigade and the gasworks people had to be called out.

The vote on the question of whether women were to

be allowed to take University degrees or not was made the occasion for another general rag. It is to be remembered that in those Victorian days of full-length skirts it was considered immodest in women to show an ankle. Opposite the Senate House a pole protruded from a window and from this pole was suspended a 'safety' bicycle. The 'safety' was then new, and the 'penny-farthing' model was dying out. On the bicycle was a life-size figure of a marvellously ugly woman in bloomers, and the whole thing bore a placard with a legend far from complimentary to the ladies. This display was only one of many of a similar sort. They were generally most ungallant, but the students of the time had determined ideas on the subject of sex equality. It is to be recorded that in the vote on the question of degrees for women the 'fair' on this occasion lost the day.

CHAPTER III

I FIND MY OCCUPATION

WHEN it became apparent that a career in Chemistry was not for me, and I had given up the idea of it in disgust, my earlier leanings towards photography influenced my choice in the matter of another job. I became a pupil for twelve months with Mr R. H. Lord, a photographer in Cambridge.

My master was a man of character with most likeable traits. He was an artist to his finger-tips, and if the 'aitches' he dropped so often turned up again in odd places, his pictures had a way of winning medals. His heart, however, was really centred on the farm he ran as a side-line. He bred collies, and his great ambition was to breed a specimen worth a hundred pounds. On his farm he had a herd of Alderney cows. So much was his mind on the farm and dairy produce that right in the middle of taking a photograph he would break off to call to his son: "Bertie! Have you sent that butter to Mrs Whosit?"

As a pupil I had many privileges. Mr Lord was a non-smoker, who did not like tobacco-smoke. It was my habit to smoke my pipe in the dark-room while he was developing, making the poor old lad cough with streaming eyes. It wasn't until he protested mildly that my "bacca would kill at a thousand yards" that I had pity on him and gave up smoking in the dark-room.

When I left Mr Lord's and Cambridge, I went as out-

38

door operator with Boughton's, a well-known firm of photographers in Lowestoft, for the season. It was a year of lovely summer, and I had what amounted to a working holiday. The week-ends I spent on the Broads with a friend. Oulton Broad was only a mile from the town, and the pair of us would hire a yawl. We had grand times in sailing, bathing, and fishing.

My next appointment was with a London firm. I was the outdoor operator, and I specialized in flashlight photography. My work took me all over London, and it kept me busy at all hours. I took photographs at theatres and dances, besides those of club groups in the daytime. I had practically a free hand and I succeeded in building up a good connexion for my firm.

The taking of flashlight photographs was a very profitable side of the business, particularly in connexion with the cheaper sort of dances—'bob hops,' and such-like affairs. It was also as amusing as it was profitable. 'The Horns' at Kennington, for example, was a great place for dancing on Saturday nights, and the hops there were to the last degree lively. It may be believed that I was, myself, ready to join at that age in any fun that was going. I had taken dancing lessons at a guinea for six at an 'Academy,' so I had little hesitation in getting on the floor when my work was done.

The Lambeth Baths was another great place for dancing at this time. During the winter the swimming-pools were boarded over and a dance-floor laid down. The Lambeth dancers were of the robuster sort who put in a lot of exercise during an evening. If it happened that a dance had words to it they exercised their lungs, too, by singing, to a man and woman, at the top of their voices. The Lambeth fancy-dress balls were marvellous for the variety and ingenuity of the costumes—anything from a haystack to a beer bottle being represented. Introductions were not considered necessary at 'hops' of this kind, and free-and-easy was the general rule. But it happened sometimes that people took part in them whose notions of etiquette were stiffer. I remember at a half-crown hop in Kensington Town Hall thinking I would take pity on a lady who seemed to be a 'wallflower.' I had seen that she had sat out during three dances, so, when the photograph had been taken, I went over to her and asked to have the pleasure of the next dance. She looked me up and down from head to heel, slowly and deliberately, then said: "I am most particular with whom I dance." " I'm not," was my prompt reply, " or I wouldn't have asked you! " And I turned away, but not before I had caught a look which, had it been as effective as it was venomous, would have slain me instantaneously.

While I was in London I was offered an appointment with the London County Council as analyst of water and gas. Three or four years previously I had applied for an appointment of such a kind, and my name had been put on the waiting list. The preliminary letter from the London County Council asked me to call at an office in Craven Street. When I arrived there, I found about a score of other applicants in attendance. They all had South Kensington Certificates in red cases under their arms, and they all were obviously eager for the position.

In they went to the examiner's sanctum, and out they came—regularly. I was the last to enter the presence of Professor Clowes.

The professor put me through a pretty stiff examination on Water Analysis. Now, I had worked from his book on Chemistry, and had always used the method of analysis evolved by himself and Coleman. But when he asked me what method I used, instead of saying ' Clowes and Coleman,' something prompted me to say ' Wanklyn.' It was not, on the face of it, a very diplomatic answer, and even now I wonder that I was told at once the job was mine. The interview took place on a Friday morning, and I was to take up the position on the Monday. This was awkward. I explained to Professor Clowes that I was in a job, and that I would have to give a week's notice. He bluntly informed me that my getting the job depended on my starting in it on the Monday. I said I should have to see my employer before I could say definitely, whereupon he gave me a stamped telegraph form and told me to wire him that very day whether I accepted or not. I was in a good deal of a quandary. In those days of thirty bob a week, the salary attached to the post was very attractive—£200 a year to start with. I had chucked up Chemistry two years previously, and I had spent quite a lot of money during my year's tuition as a photographer; it was time that something happened.

I went back to the studio and told my boss all about it. " If you want to go I will not stand in your way," was his immediate comment. I asked his advice, but he refused to urge me either way. We argued pros and cons for about a couple of hours, but I could get no help from him in making a decision. I could not make up my mind, and at length, " All right," I said, " I'll toss for it— heads I accept; tails I refuse." Up went the coin. It came down tails up. I wrote out the wire refusing the job and sent it off at once by the apprentice. That gambling decision, as you will see, had quite an effect on my life.

Shortly after my refusal of the L.C.C. position I was offered another with the Wiltshire County Council, as assistant to the Medical Officer of Health. The fact that I had refused the L.C.C. job, as if out of preference for sticking to photography, made it seem silly to accept this second offer, and I refused it.

I did not stay much longer with that first London firm and my next job was with a Court photographer in Kensington. Then I went as manager to a business in Norwich, and while there I received an offer from a firm of chemists to go to Rhodesia, to open a photographic department in Bulawayo.

This offer I accepted.

CHAPTER IV

SOUTHWARD HO!

IT was on a miserably cold and damp October afternoon that I arrived in Southampton to embark on the old *Dunottar Castle*.

A gale was blowing, and no sooner had we got out into the Channel than the tyros aboard—myself included—began to learn what a storm at sea was like. Waves were breaking over the upper decks; all the movable gear above board was lashed for security; below the fiddles were in use, and all port-holes were screwed tight shut. The old ship, pitching and rolling at the same time, had something of a corkscrew motion, but the roll on her was particularly remarkable. She would heel over until it seemed that she would never right again. One held one's breath, expecting to be upside down next minute, but she would slowly straighten, only to repeat the heavy cant in the other direction.

Of the hundreds of passengers aboard only three turned out for dinner. For myself, I was not at all eager for food, but I did manage to absorb some sustenance. It did not do me much good, however. After dinner I went on deck, and to the crash of the waves and the music of the sea I rendered up what I had absorbed. This was the only meal I lost on the voyage. Pray notice that this was after I'd had it.

On our first morning out the sea was still very rough, and of the solitary two who appeared for breakfast I was one. Very few of the passengers turned out for meals until Madeira was reached, though some of the convalescents took broth and tea on deck, fearful of moving in case of accident. It was " Any more for the mop? " with most of them.

At Madeira there were the usual activities: throwing pennies for the natives to dive after, bargaining for Madeira wares, fine lace work, wicker-chairs, and so forth. Five of us made up a party to go ashore, all men. We went up the mountain by train and had breakfast on the peak. It was a splendid meal of fresh fish and fruit, with wonderful scenery on which to feast the eyes at the same time. After that came the rush down the mountain-side over cobble-stones on the toboggan affairs peculiar to Madeira. Half-way down the natives who controlled the toboggans in pairs called a halt. It may be or may not be accounted an odd circumstance—according to the fancy of the reader—that the halt was called immediately in front of a wine shop. It seemed, in any case, to be the recognized practice to stoke-up the guides. Ultimately we got to the town of Funchal. There was the usual pestering by guides, with the usual simulacrum of a free fight and the usual unsimulated pandemonium until one was chosen. Then we wandered round the town seeing the usual sights and having the usual rides on the bullock-drawn sleds.

At the first opportunity afforded us for drawing normal breath the five men who composed the party fell to comparing notes. We discovered that, by curious coincidence, all five of us were bound for Rhodesia—a coincidence made all the more curious by the later discovery that we were the only passengers aboard making for that destination. The stop at Madeira concluded, we were off again, *en route* for Cape Town. And now the weather was splendid, giving all the passengers a chance to find sea-legs.

There were, it may be stated, one or two voyagers in the ship whom the normal among us remarked as being quaint. One of our 'characters' was a Dutchman who had been in England for a two months' trip, and who was going back to his dorp at Malmesbury to write a book on England and the English. The Boer War was in progress, and a little group of us found amusement in pulling the Dutchman's leg. He could play the piano, and so was often called upon to accompany singers. A favourite song of the period was *The Admiral's Broom*, in which, it may be remembered, the protagonists are Admirals Blake and Van Tromp, with the climax of the story not so favourable for the latter. There was peculiar titillation for the larky ones among us in watching our Dutchman solemnly thumping out the tune without the faintest notion of the meaning of the words. Among the liveliest of our sparks aboard were four or five Scotsmen, lads up to any caper. One of them in an argument happened to call the pianist " a bloody Dutchman." The Dutchman was considerably annoyed about it, and threatened to report the matter to the Captain. " Hoo-oots, too-oots, man! " drawled one of the Scots. " If Ah was to report to the Captain every time onybody ca'd me a bluidy Scotsman, Ah'd be up an' doon the bridge-ladder a' day! "

There was one passenger I remember who was of the chosen race, and who bore the name 'Jesus Christ.' But

45

he pronounced his second name as though it rhymed with 'wrist.'

We had the usual ceremonies on crossing the Line, with Father Neptune in charge. There were the usual crude barberings, in which, of course, the old paint-brush was greatly in evidence, and duckings were numerous. But, in the soldier's phrase, a good time was had by all; the whole voyage, after sea-legs were found, could hardly have been jollier. I was just of an age then to get all the fun out of it a young fellow would.

The end of the voyage was like the end of all voyages. The night before we arrived in Table Bay all was excitement. The particular pals of the voyage arranged meetings. Autographs and addresses were exchanged, with the usual vows of eternal friendship; but we may suppose without undue cynicism that after the passage of a few letters those vows and ship-friendships fell into the limbo of forgetfulness. With the dawn came Cape Town, and a picture to remember—the town lying cool and serene at the foot of Table Mountain, while above, the Table-cloth of white cloud was spread over the mountain-top, the peak only breaking through.

The port officials and clearing agents came aboard and got through their duties, and at last the impatient passengers were permitted to land. I was in no hurry, and was finding much interest in watching disembarkation operations from the upper deck. Suddenly I was hailed by name from the shore. Looking down, I saw an old friend from my own town, Cambridge, a man called George Branch. I had not known he was in Africa. "Hullo, Clark! Is it yourself?" "Myself in person," said I, and made my way to the quayside to shake him by the hand. What with his eagerness for news of the old place and my own desire to extract impressions of this, to me, new country, it may be conceived how our tongues wagged.

Some time after this I was on my way to Rondebosch to meet a married cousin whom I had not seen since my perambulator days. Fellow-passengers were with me part of the way, but got off at Salt river, not far out of the town. They had no sooner left than a fellow sitting in a far corner of the carriage said: " Hullo, Clark! " " Why, Sago! " I returned in surprise. It was a fellow I had been at school with in Cambridge. He was trooper in Brabant's Horse, down from the Front on leave. It did look as if I could not escape contacts with the old town—not that I wanted to.

Before I could leave for the north I had to obtain a travelling permit from the Castle, but thanks to the Chartered Company's agent I had little trouble. Before I left I went to see a friend of mine, manager of a bank in Cape Town. He took it upon himself to give me advice. " My boy," he said, " you are going to Rhodesia; you'll find everybody there gambling in stocks and shares. Take my advice and cut all that out." Well, I did take his advice. I have never indulged in gambling of that sort. But not long afterwards I heard that my adviser had shot himself rather than face heavy liabilities he had incurred in the very speculation he had warned me against.

As a matter of fact, the only gambling of this kind I ever did was when I got to Bulawayo. I bought a Prospector's Licence for a shilling, and sold it for a pound to a friend immediately I got out of the office.

47

Eventually I set out for Rhodesia. The five of us who had discovered each other in the *Dunottar Castle* went on the same train to Bulawayo. In those days there were no dining-cars on the trains, and we had to take our own nose-bags. At various stations along the line stops were made nominally to give time for meals at the refreshment rooms. Tickets for those meals were issued on the trains *en route*. The refreshment rooms were all owned by one man. Twenty minutes were allowed for the meals, but owing to the large number of passengers and the limited catering provision it was a job to get served. Popular theory had it that the soup of the first course was served at boiling point so that by the time it had cooled enough to be swallowed a rush had to be made for the train, and the further courses of the meal had to be left untouched. The theory was, perhaps, a humorous exaggeration of the actual difficulties that stood between train-travellers and food, but one did have to get along on short commons just as surely as if it had been true.

From De Aar on the journey northward we were attended by an armoured train. No travelling was done at night. The farther north we went the more block-houses were in evidence. During stops Tommies went along the train asking for news of home or for papers, and picking up cigarette-ends. They were very short, poor beggars, of even the minor luxuries. Not that they ever asked for cigarettes or things of that sort, but the sight of them hunting for fag-ends made many a cigarette packet go down to them. At Modder river there was a sight to evoke all one's pity in the row upon row of graves of soldiers fallen in the war, and in the row upon row of crosses made from railway sleepers that stood at their heads. In lesser number the graves and crosses were to be seen at intervals along the line. A large number of the graves held men not dead in battle but who had died of enteric, for the toll of fever in the Boer War was tremendous. Just before we reached Kimberley we passed a long train taking Boer prisoners to Cape Town. The escort of soldiers in ragged khaki, unshaven and unshorn, was as disreputable-looking a gang as I have ever seen. It was discovered, when our train stopped in a siding alongside this prisoners' train, that the escort was of the Household Cavalry, the Blues. Someone in our train called out: " What price Knightsbridge? " And the answer came back promptly: " My Gawd! Don't I wish I was there now! " At Kimberley we replenished our nose-bags.

Mafeking, farther on, was an abomination of desolation. The whole town was in ruins, what houses there were left half-standing by the shell-fire being full of holes. One marvelled how the place had withstood the siege. From the nature of the surrounding country it looked as if the taking of Mafeking should have been easy, since it was held by such a small force. But the genius of the Boers in fighting was not in close work or the use of the bayonet, but in open warfare.

We travelled, as I have said, in the day-time only. There was too much danger in moving at night. So much of our progress was through what practically was enemy country, and the line might be torn up or the train wrecked by explosives. Altogether, with one thing and another, it took us seven days' weary travelling to get to Bulawayo. Until I began to travel myself I had thought Cambridge folk stayed at home. But at Bulawayo I was

D

met by another Cambridge friend, Harold Smart, and taken by him to see still another, Ellis Allen.

Bulawayo at this time was a tin town containing few buildings of any pretension. My employers, for whom I was to open a photographic department, could give me only the poorest accommodation. My quarters were in an out-house built of wood and iron, used mainly as a packing-shed. The dark-room, in the middle, was about the size of a telephone-box, and my own first dark-room with the lamp burning was an ice-box compared to this. The shed itself was hot, but the dark-room was an oven, and I was drenched with perspiration after ten minutes in it. The whole photographic department, in fact, was replete with every inconvenience. Printing was done in the open. The toning and fixing of photos was a chancy job because of the dust. This penetrated every-where, and dust-storms were frequent. During the season one often read notices on the business houses: " Closed on account of dust."

There are two seasons in Bulawayo, the rainy and the dry. In the rainy season, those days, one carried Bula-wayo around on one's boots; in the dry, one carried it all over one, in the eyes, nose, mouth, and hair—hence the thirst that one knew from early morn till dewy eve. And, alas! the 'dew' wasn't always there. Nowadays the 'dust-devil' has been greatly suppressed in the town itself with the macadamizing of the streets. One of the fine features of the main streets is their ample width. This was due to Cecil Rhodes. He wanted thoroughfares in which a wagon with a span of sixteen oxen could turn comfortably. And dusty and unmade though they were,

A DUST-DEVIL AT BULAWAYO

they were illuminated by arc lamps at a time when the streets of most English towns were lit by gas.

But the changes in Bulawayo in my time, as may be imagined, have been very great. The thirty-foot store of wood and iron which was occupied by Messrs Haddon and Sly has given place to palatial premises. The small building which housed Messrs Meikles, Ltd., is now a tremendous departmental store. In a little tin shanty Major Charles Duly sold bicycles. His motor business is now one of the biggest in the country, with buildings in proportion, and, like the firms above mentioned, it has branches in other towns.

When I arrived in Rhodesia, it should be remembered, it had been on the map only six or seven years, but it was already getting into its stride. I was one of the very few male inhabitants who were not, or had not been, in the British South African Police—familiarly, the B.S.A.P. I was a greenhorn among those fellows, but I took to Rhodesian life straightaway. Its ease and freedom and its air of happy-go-lucky suited me very well.

My first lodgings was a room in chambers opposite the gaol, a choice, you may be sure, which gave the older hands opportunity for rude remarks. Sitting out on the veranda—in the rainy season, it was—reading by electric light, I became speedily acquainted with the multitude of different insects that the country swarmed with. And I am ready to admit that I was scared stiff. There were beetles large and small, moths, and other winged creatures of hateful character.

The rhino beetles were as big in the body as half a crown. With horns on their snouts they would buzz along and strike one, blunderingly, in the face. The impact hurt, but that was their worst injury. Smaller beetles, on the other hand, found lodgment in one's hair or inside one's shirt, driving one almost daft. The loathliest of the small ones was the stink beetle, an insect the size of a lady-bird. This creature, when instinctively pulled off the skin or squashed under the shirt, left on one the most putrid of smells which did not vanish in several washings. The Christmas beetles filled the air with a shrill penetrating whistle that could be heard a mile away. The tarantulas that roamed around, large pink repulsive spiders, filled me with fear and disgust. Then there were scorpions on occasion. They had the appearance of little black lobsters, and their sting, which I suffered three times, caused great swelling and pain for a week or two. Besides all these beasties, there were centipedes.

In the Matjumschlope, a river not far from my quarters, frogs kept up an incessant chorus, from the deep croakings of the old bull frogs through the varying notes of differing ages to the lighter tones of the youngest generation. It was a chorus heard all night and every night, but I learned to ignore it.

On a morning soon after my arrival in Bulawayo the brightness of the day was suddenly darkened by the passing of a black cloud over the sun. It was a cloud covering an area of several miles. Clamour immediately arose; the hellish din of paraffin cans and tin trays being frantically beaten. The cloud was of locusts, and the noise was made to prevent them settling, for where they settle they leave no vegetation uneaten. The row was effective; the locusts passed over the town.

It was in this early period of my stay in Bulawayo that

George Walton's Comedy Company came to the town. The Company gave its performance in the Empire Theatre, an oblong building capable of seating some two hundred people. To make a performance at all profitable the prices of admission had of course to be high. I interviewed George Walton and arranged to take a flashlight photograph of the stage and the players from the body of the hall. This was the first flashlight photograph to be taken in Southern Rhodesia. The following night, just before the beginning of the show, I visited George in his dressing-room and let him see a proof copy of the photograph. He stared at the picture, then shouted to his wife in the next dressing-room. She came in and had a look at the proof. " This," she said, " is the best flashlight I've ever seen—bar one." I asked her where this excepted picture was taken. "At the first performance at the Kennington Theatre," Mary Walton replied; " I was playing principal boy." " Well, I took that picture too," I said. They were astonished at the coincidence, but were convinced of my veracity when I named the manager, Jack Donald, and the pantomime, *Cinderella*, with other circumstances attached to the Kennington performance.

This was not the only coincidence connected with my acquaintance with George Walton. I had gone with members of the Company on a picnic to the Umgusa river, some four or five miles from Bulawayo, and a splendid time we had. George and I went for a stroll. It was a very hot day and, after a time, fed-up, weary, and dripping with perspiration, George sat down beside a discovery notice, or claim-plate for a mine, which we came upon, and I took a photograph of him. When I

53

gave him a print of this he was tickled to find that the claim-plate bore the legend: " George Walton Reef."

I did not stay very long in my quarters opposite the gaol. My next lodging was a room in a house at the end of Fort Street. This was quite a mile out of town, with but few houses in the distance between. The brick-fields were near by, and my new room was practically on the veldt. I stayed here about a couple of months.

One Saturday I had been in town for an evening at cards. It was about midnight when I left my friends and set out for home. My road lay straight before me, but it was pitch dark and rain was beginning. I had no lantern—and this was in the days before electric torches. The darkness was a blanket over my head. A quarter of a mile out the rain came down in one solid sheet. I could not see a yard in front of me, and, missing my road completely, I was soon lost in the veldt. For a couple of hours I wandered about, lost in the pelting rain. Not a house could I discover, nor any landmark. I could not tell where the next step would take me. At last, about two o'clock in the morning, I saw a light in the distance, and I made for it. As I neared it I saw it came from a hut standing solitary in the veldt. In answer to my knocking the door was opened by a man who sported a wild beard that made him look more like a bushranger than anything else. He had a shot-gun at the ready in his hands. " What the blankety blank-blank do you want? " he demanded. " Would you mind directing me to Bula-wayo? " said I. " I have lost my way." " Foot-sack to hell out of it," was the obliging reply, " or you'll get a load of buck-shot into you! " There was no use arguing. I simply foot-sacked!

Wet, weary, and worn, I plodded once again through the mirk and rain, still without any idea of my direction, till once again I saw a light. Full of hope I made for it, to find it came from one of several houses in a cluster. I was approaching the house that showed the light, when a couple of ferocious dogs rushed at me. Once more argument was useless. I retreated backward, waving my hat at them, till the night and the rain covered me.

At long last I saw a building. It looked to me like the familiar Market Hall, and I fixed my eyes on it and moved briskly towards it. It was looming up grandly when suddenly I stepped into a sluit full of water and fell down smack. The sousing, however, added nothing to the drenched condition I was in, and I crawled out in the direction of the building. Judge of my surprise when I found that I had reached my own dwelling, quite a mile away from the Market Hall I had thought the building was. It was four o'clock in the morning. Never was my bed so welcome. I slept like a top.

The next day I went to have a look at the Matjumschlope river. It had risen so many feet in the night that its waters were over the bridge that crossed it. This is by no means an uncommon phenomenon; a Rhodesian rain-storm must be experienced ere one can get an idea of the downpour in which I had wandered through the night, a stranger in a strange land.

A few days before my night adventure I'd had my first introduction to a tropical storm. It began with a hurricane of wind that blew off the roofs of several houses. I saw the roof of a brick pavilion lifted like the top of an egg and carried away, and a hut blown bodily down the street like a sheet of paper. Then came the hail, with stones as big as marbles. After that, the rain. In half an hour it registered one and a half inches. At the time I fancied I was seeing the noted tropical rain, but my night in the veldt gave me a better idea of the potentialities.

There was fun as well as woe in those early days in Rhodesia. I remember the pleasure and enjoyment of my first Christmas, which was spent on the veldt.

I was invited to join a party going to camp in the Matoppos near the ' World's View,' the place selected by Cecil Rhodes for his tomb. It was an invitation that, as may be imagined, I eagerly accepted. The party was to consist of two married couples and four single men and we were to trek by mule wagon. Our luck in this last regard was in, for the organizer of the trip, Charlie Maton, was in the transport section of the B.S.A.P., and so was able to borrow ten mules and a light tent wagon.

We started off gaily enough in lovely weather. The distance to our first outspan from Bulawayo was twenty-eight miles, but the track was not always easy to find, and by the time it was dark we were off the trail. We outspanned, however, shortly after dusk, having found a pool of water near a Kaffir kraal. From this we drew water for our coffee and the qualifying of other liquid refreshment, and again for our coffee in the early morning. With the dawning our mules were inspanned, and by six o'clock we were on our way again.

It happened that I looked back while we still were in sight of the pool. What I saw there made me suggest

56

that the rest of the party should look back too. They saw, as I had seen, about a dozen niggers having their morning dip in the pool. Like the august lady of the story, the party was " not amused " !

Our route now led us through rock scenery of great magnificence. Kopjes and isolated rocks of huge size dotted the landscape, some of the tremendous rocks perched with such seeming peril on the tops of others that they looked as though they might come thundering down at any moment. The rocks were girt by trees and shrubs, magnificent in their many shades of green and in the lovely blooms and pods of all colours that decorated them. This was untouched Nature; it was deeply impressive.

Soon after our start we arrived at a place where a dam was being built. It was in an early stage of its construction, with, apparently, neither road nor track to permit us to get round it. There was, however, a very narrow track above the dam that seemed to go in our desired direction, and this we decided to risk. The venture was not to be without peril, it seemed, for our host got all the passengers off the wagon. Walking did not appeal to my adventurous spirit, and I urged Charlie to let me go with him. After some persuasion he consented. I was to hold the mules until they got started, then I was to hop on the wagon's stern. At the word of command I gave the mules their heads. In my excitement I failed to get wide enough of the wagon and a wheel went over my foot. Still, I contrived to get aboard and hold on. Charlie had set off at a gallop, I suppose, because it was as easy to go fast as slowly. It was a mercy that he did keep the mules at the gallop, for half-way along one of the wheels went over the edge of the declivity, and only our speed prevented us from going over.

By the track's end we came on some huts. The occupants told us that there actually was a road round the dam, and that nobody had ever driven by the path we had chosen. They marvelled that we had got through, especially with a wagon and ten mules. " Fools for luck," the saying goes. In proportion to the luck we had that morning we were fools indeed.

At 8.30 A.M. we arrived at our destination, and the men made camp while the ladies prepared breakfast. Right from that moment the game of befooling the greenhorn (myself) commenced. There was no end to the dodges invented for pulling my leg.

One of the party, an enormous fellow, advised me that for climatic reasons I should take ' Eno's ' every morning, and he offered to start me off with a handful of the salts. His hand was like a leg of mutton, and his handful tremendous. I was innocent enough to accept his ' kindness ' at its face value, and took the handful at one go. Without descending into details I will merely say that I betook me into the veldt, to remain there for two hours, and to return tottering to find somewhere to lie down. Believe me, I slept the sleep of the exhausted until sounds of chanting awoke me. A procession of white-clad figures was passing solemnly round my bed to the strains of the Dead March in *Saul*. Round and round they marched, varying the dirge with recitations from the Burial Service, till I started heaving rocks at them, when my tormentors left me alone.

The breaking-in process went on, and I was not a stupid pupil.

At night the mules were tethered to trees with sufficient lengths of rope to give them fair grazing space. We dined close to where they were tethered, and I fed with my back to the animals. One of the brutes, trying, I think, to knock a fly off his rump, missed his aim and landed a hoof on me. The kick was not an especially hard one, but I put it down in my accounts under the general heading ' Education.'

To this account too goes down my choice of a nice smooth rock as a couch on retiring that night. Before morning I had learned that rocks are unyielding and my anatomy full of knobs. My hips, shoulders, elbows, and other projections ached abominably, and I was cruelly in want of sleep. It taught me one of the primary lessons of sleeping in the open—to seek sand in which hollows can be made to accommodate one's major protuberances.

I could not have had my initiation into life out of doors in Rhodesia under happier circumstances. The lovely weather, although the trip was made in the middle of the rainy season, held for the four days the picnic lasted. As I say, I learned rapidly, and the jokes played on me and my greenhorn mishaps were taken philosophically as material of experience. Even the ' Eno's ' trick helped me to wariness. I can say without reservations that my first Christmas in Rhodesia was a great success.

When the time came to inspan for the return journey we all got aboard and set off upon a road that was everywhere rough and in parts rocky. We were jolting along, at about ten miles an hour, when suddenly there was really a monster jerk. The passengers, one and all, rose bodily and of no volition from their seats into the air.

59

Charlie Maton, driving, was chucked forward clean over the footboard and fell between the wagon-front and the wheeler mules. Fortunately, he came to ground on his feet, and to keep himself from being run over he had to trot between the wagon and the sterns of the mules. I was on the driving-seat and managed to gather up the reins, but Charlie had to trot a good fifty yards before I could pull up. Thus the funniest incident of the picnic happened towards its end, and for once it wasn't I who afforded the sport. I can recall nothing so comic as the picture of Charlie trotting, forced, willy-nilly, to keep in step with the wheeler mules.

On the journey out and home we came across many stern reminders of the hazards that settlers in the country had so often to face. Two years previously there had been a visitation of the rinderpest, which had killed off thousands of head, not only of cattle, but of game. Horns and bones lay bleached all about the veldt, saddening us with thoughts of the huge losses suffered by the farmers.

CHAPTER V

ROUGH DOINGS

IN the early part of 1901 an epidemic of enteric broke out in the camp of the British South African Police. Every day while it lasted a procession of the police was to be seen slow marching with reversed arms to the sob of muffled drums. The outbreak had taken sad toll of the troopers, many a fine fellow being cut off in the prime of life before the cause of the disease was found. It then appeared that the well from which the police camp drew its water was contaminated by the dead body of a native who had fallen into it weeks previously.

I did not escape the scourge myself, but it wasn't water from the police well that gave it me. I'm inclined to think a dead python had something to do with it—a large reptile which had been brought in for pickling. The receptacle containing it was just outside the place where I worked. During the pickling process the container somehow got partly uncovered, and with the heat of the sun the fluid naturally evaporated, exposing the carcase. In a few days the stench was horrible. My complaints were met by promises that the offence would be removed " to-morrow," but that ' to-morrow '—like so many—did not come.

One morning I awoke feeling very ill indeed. I sent my boy to the warehouse with a message that I would not be turning up that day. Five days elapsed during which I lay sick, then a member of the firm came to see me. He called in a doctor, who promptly had me taken off to hospital. No private wards were available, and I was put into a four-bed ward.

I lay for the first two weeks watching screens being put up round the other beds. In the middle of the night orderlies would come in, and in the morning a screen would be gone and the bed empty.

One day a nurse came to me and began to deposit ice-bags about my middle.

" What's that for, Nurse? " I asked.

" Oh, to keep you cool," was the reply—but I wasn't fooled.

" You think I don't know," I said, " but I reckon it's internal hæmorrhage—what? "

" You know too much," said the nurse. " Shut up! "

Well, a few days later the screen enclosed my bed, and late that night the doctor and matron came in. Whether they thought I was asleep or unconscious I don't know, but I heard part of their conversation after they moved away from looking at me. In a feeble voice I called the matron.

" Matron," I said, " you think I'm going to peg out— but I don't! "

Nor did I, as you see. But the doctor told me afterwards that I would have done no less if I had worried at all.

During the time that I lay most helpless a man was brought in and put to bed. We were the only two patients at that time in the ward. At tea time, when we were unattended, the newcomer hopped out of bed and went to the window. In a most excited manner he described realistically a murder that was going on in the hospital grounds. He recorded every detail of the supposed murder, and I could do nothing to stem the spate of graphic description. I was too weak to reach the bell to summon a nurse.

Later, however, a nurse did come in and got him back to bed. Her name was Williams, I remember, and she handled him wonderfully. I called her over and told her what had happened. He was removed to a private ward, but I could hear him shouting and yelling for a long time afterwards.

That same night, when he was left alone for a few minutes, the madman jumped clean through a window. Nurse Williams went after him and managed to overtake him close to the Police camp. Shouting for help, she tackled him alone. Help came, and the fellow was secured and taken back to hospital. It was a marvellously plucky thing that Nurse Williams did; the man was in the middle of a bad attack of delirium tremens.

With convalescence the worst of my trials, as I considered it, began. For a fortnight after I regained normal temperature I was allowed no solid food. The other patients were getting food, and the smell of it almost drove me frantic—so frantic that the driest of bread would have been wolfed at once. The time came, however, when I was allowed bread and milk—a very small serving. It happened that when I got this ration the nurses were changing guard, and by mistake I was brought a second helping. Ravenous, I concealed the fact that I'd already had my allowance, and I got outside the second supply—pronto! But Nemesis was waiting by my elbow. Very soon I was in agony and convinced for the first time in my illness that my last hour had come. It served me right, I suppose, for cheating.

On my discharge from hospital I went to a small hotel at Forest Vale, four miles out of town, to recuperate. After a fortnight there I felt fairly fit and thought myself ready for home. The landlord of the hotel offered me a lift into town, but I refused. I said I would walk. It was about four in the afternoon when I set out, but it was seven before I reached the outskirts of Bulawayo. I had found myself so much weaker than I had imagined. I had to stagger into the house of a friend for a long rest before I was fit to be helped the rest of the way home.

I went back to business, but did not pick up. A good part of each day was spent in lying down. It was then found that I had a bad attack of jaundice, and I was again consigned to bed for a week or two. I simply could not keep awake.

It will be gathered that experience was coming to me fast.

Shortly after I got over my second ailment I joined with Ellis Allen, a friend from Cambridge, in taking over a four-roomed house on the outskirts of the town. It was not until we had been several days in occupation that we learned that the previous tenant had committed suicide. This explained the cheap rental on which we had taken the house over. I cannot say that the knowledge worried either of us any, and we certainly were not bothered by ghosts.

If we had any worry at all, it was to keep warm o'

nights. Though the days were as bright and sunny as those of an English summer, the nights were bitterly cold.

We solved the problem of firing with rather youthful unscrupulousness. Next door to us lived a couple of men who ran a considerable engineering business, and in their backyard was an enormous pile of firewood collected from the veldt. My friend and I took it in turn night about to appropriate as much wood as we needed from the engineers' pile. We never went cold—and we never were caught. There was more devilment than nefarious-ness in this unseemly activity, because we could have collected far more wood than we needed from the same source as our neighbours at negligible cost. When by and by we did confess our sinning to the Johnnies next door they were highly amused, and the debt was liqui-dated with the standing of a drink or so.

It would be about this time that there took place, as I remember it, one of those cases peculiar in unsavoury detail to the place and time. A native raped a white woman and mutilated her fearfully. He was captured and brought to court.

The first day of the trial was occupied in taking evi-dence, which was not completed when the court ad-journed. To some of the citizens the process seemed unduly long-drawn, and at a meeting of the more impatient of them it was decided that as soon as the verdict was given against the prisoner—it being considered a foregone conclusion that the verdict could go no other way—he was to be seized and executed summarily. Not far from the court-house, and right opposite the Bulawayo Club, there was a fine large

E   65

electric standard. It was decided that nothing could be more suitable for a gallows.

Next day the verdict did go against the prisoner. It was no sooner uttered than the ready group behind the dock had a rope about his neck and had hauled him bodily over the dock's edge. The magistrate hastily left the bench and ran down the court-room to protest. But something happened to the dignitary which left him *hors de combat* for the rest of the proceedings. The native was dragged by the rope about his neck towards the lamp-post, but the progress was so delayed, on account of the gathering of the crowd which was keen to partake in wreaking spite upon him, that arrival at the improvised gallows coincided with the advent of a contingent of the B.S.A.P. The police rescued the prisoner, and later the death penalty by hanging—which still is the fate of natives convicted of rape—was executed upon him by the competent authorities.

This incident illustrates primitive life as it is everywhere in a young country with a native population preponderating largely over a sprinkling of white. Nothing makes the blood of the settler seethe like the mere thought of racial contamination. And not only in cases such as I have quoted. I could tell true tales of white women of easy virtue being tarred and feathered for consorting with blacks, but I won't. There are rough enough things to tell of that may be more amusing.

Life was rough in Rhodesia then in more senses than one, but I was rapidly shaking down to acceptance of it. I was beginning to get used even to the high prices

66

HANGING SPIES IN THE MAIN STREET OF BULAWAYO DURING THE MATABELE REBELLION, 1896

of commodities, and to find amusement in the astonishment of newcomers at first acquaintance with them. When I tell you that eggs, for example, were ten shillings a dozen in my first days, cabbages four shillings each, and beer four shillings a bottle, you will gather that the dismay of newcomers could be funny enough.

A new assistant of the firm I worked for was to arrive from England, and three of my cronies and myself went to meet him at the station, a mile out of town. For the first night it was arranged that he should be accommodated at the hotel. The newcomer had a lot of luggage, and he naturally thought of a cab. A cab was secured, and all five of us bundled into it. On arrivel at the hotel our new chum had his first shock. The cabby demanded fifteen shillings for the mile ride—and got it. We old hands, of course, betrayed neither astonishment nor amusement. We conducted the new chum into the bar. Since we had done him the honour of meeting him it was unnecessary openly to moot the notion that he should put up a round of drinks. All we had to do was to conduct him to the bar—and wait. His second shock came when he had to fork out. Twelve-and-six for the round, it was. He just managed to survive the second lesson in his Rhodesian education.

Newcomers were usually initiated at the Palace hotel, but we had another in the town, the Grand. This was considered one of our show-places, and it was, for the period, quite an imposing building. A gentleman whose natural tongue, I believe, was Yiddish was the proprietor. Rumour arose that he was selling liquor which did not meet with the promise given by the proprietary labels on the bottles, and when the truth of the rumour was established, a vengeful crowd of the B.S.A.P. surged in upon him one night, broke up half the stock of bottles in the place, smashed plate-glass windows and mirrors and a lot of furniture, pretty well wrecking the bar. The ringleaders in this exploit were discovered and arrested. They were brought to trial, and two of them were sentenced to imprisonment.

I had a great friend at this time who was a trooper in the force to which the bar-smashers belonged. His name was O'Connor, an Irish-American, blue-eyed and handsome, and a man of great charm. Soon after our friendship developed he left the B.S.A.P. and found a job with an auctioneer. One morning when we were out for a stroll it chanced that our conversation passed to the subject of fighting. " Do you know, P.M.," said O'Connor, " I haven't had a scrap for ages."

" No more have I," said I.

" Well," said O'Connor, with that winning smile of his, " what about one now? "

" I'm game."

Thereupon we retired to the back premises of a saddler, and the man of leather agreed to referee. There was another fellow who looked on. Then began a marvellous set-to with bare fists. I can't and couldn't fight for nuts, and O'Connor could put two hundred pounds behind his punches. They were like the kicks of an army mule. Still, I did manage to black his eye in return for the split ear he gave me in the early stages of the fight. The contest lasted many rounds, and ended with O'Connor having both his eyes blackened and myself one. But then, as makeweight, I had the slit ear. The fight was conducted in a friendly spirit, neither of us losing our tempers. What stopped the fight was the discovery that we were hungry and that it was time for lunch.

Next door to the saddler's was a small restaurant, and we went there. In the middle of lunch O'Connor expressed dissatisfaction with the fight. It appeared to him that the results were unequal, he having two black eyes to my one. He thought we ought to finish it off properly. " What do you say, P.M.? "

" I'm agreeable," I said.

So once more we adjourned to the backyard and set to. This time, however, the contest did not last long. O'Connor slipped and went down, spraining his ankle. I helped him to his room, and he had to lie up for several days. The scrap, as I say, was absolutely friendly, and we both enjoyed it. A daft proceeding, if you like, but we were no madder in this than were most of the young men of our age at that time and in that place.

A few years ago now, and some thirty years after that scrap, I was sitting with a friend and some other men on the veranda of the Victoria Falls hotel. I had known my friend very well for over twenty years, please note. Suddenly, as we were sitting there, he turned to me and said, out of the blue: " Do you remember, P.M., that fight you had with O'Connor in the saddler's yard at Bulawayo? "

" I remember," I replied. " What do you know about it? "

" I saw it," he said. " It was the finest scrap I've ever seen."

Then I remembered the fourth chap, the onlooker at the fight. This friend of twenty years' standing was he, but it was the first time he had mentioned the scrap between O'Connor and me. I should mention that we once had lived together at the Old Drift for twelve months on end. Well, now—how's that for reticence?

The bars in Bulawayo closed at eleven P.M., but if one needed refreshment after hours there were tea-rooms that kept open half the night. Going home with O'Connor once in the small hours he asked me what my reaction was to the idea of a night-cap. I said that my reaction was favourable but that the idea was useless, the bars being closed. Without further argument he took me, as it were, by the hand, led me to one of those tea-rooms, and ordered a cup of tea apiece—" with a stick in it." We were promptly served with whisky and soda in teacups. Of course, only the known friends of the house could procure this special brand of tea, but O'Connor was the sort of chap who knew all the dodges. Much of the education I have mentioned came to me from him. But the whisky in the teacup dodge goes to show that even then and in that rough town liquor restrictions only led to the ' shebeen,' or pioneer form of ' speak-easy.'

A war scare about this time made a soldier of me for a while. It was reported that the Boers were upon us; they had been seen quite near. A meeting was called in haste at the Charter Hotel, resulting in the formation of a Town Guard. Five companies were made up, and rifles and ammunition were issued by the authorities, together with hats, bandoliers, and other equipment. The Boers did not, as it happened, materialize, but the defence force thus formed put in a lot of company drills and practised shooting in orthodox style. For the latter purpose ranges were constructed in various places. My mob was called the Hillside Troop, and was commanded by Captain Bourchier Wrey. Marking at the ranges was done for us by professionals, privates in the K.O.S.B. who wanted to earn a bob or two. The Scottish Borderers were stationed in Bulawayo at this time. The regiment's reputation for toughness was of old standing even then, and the men lived up to it. Their favourite weapon in a ' rough-house ' was their belt, which was of leather in those days, with a heavy buckle. It was the buckle-end they used in a ' free-for-all.'

The Hillside Troop in which I did my bit of soldiering took its name from the district where I shared a house with Ellis Allen. The house was built of brick and it stood some three and a half miles out of Bulawayo. It was owned by that magistrate who got hurt in the rumpus over the native previously mentioned. It stood in grounds of three acres, with outhouses and all the usual conveniences.

The Hillside district at this time was very sparsely built on. There were only about half a dozen houses all told, and the lonely situation encouraged the visits of prowlers looking for anything that could be ' lifted.' Allen and myself were visited more than once, and we agreed that if either of us heard suspicious noises in the night he was to wake the other. Together we were to make for the front door, leave it simultaneously, and proceed at a run in opposite directions round the house. Each of us was armed with a fine specimen of knob-kerry—that native mace of hardwood with a heavy round end.

71

The plan looked all right in projection, but we discovered in the first working of it that it could easily be perilous in ways unforeseen. I had rushed to the back of the house, according to plan, and was kneeling to try for a view of the supposed intruder against the skyline. Allen, turning the corner, spotted my crouching figure, and was just on the point of giving me the weight of his knobkerry when he discovered my identity. Even now I cannot recall that escape without a feeling of uneasiness, for Allen was notably impetuous and would not have spared a suspected intruder.

The next occasion was funnier, if not less scaring at the time. Sounds outside my bedroom window aroused me—peculiar sounds. I woke Allen up, got with him to the front door, and bolted round the house in the arranged direction. At the corner of the house, going at full speed, I went bang into an obstacle which seemed to be as solid as the house itself. A mule had strayed into our grounds and was having a good feed off the creeper that grew up the sides of the house.

Life was full of incident in those early days, and some of the things we did were not so creditable as they seemed amusing in our young idea. Not far from where I lived with Ellis Allen three other fellows kept house. Often of a Saturday night I would join these three fellows in their *kia* for a game of cards. Allen did not play cards, so he had no share in the trick I'm coming to. The card parties frequently went on into the dawn, when, with the break-up of the ' school,' a whisky and milk was indicated. It happened as often as not that there would be no milk in the house.

Fortunately, however—or unfortunately, if you like,

from the viewpoint that need and opportunity combine to create the crime—the next-door neighbour of my three friends kept a cow. One of the card-party was an expert milker. With the aid of a bucket and a little stealth he had small difficulty in securing us an ample supply. The owner of the cow was puzzled to make out why on so many Sunday mornings the animal was dry, but concluded that snakes were the thieves.

There were, indeed, plenty of snakes around, and I became expert in spotting and killing them quickly. But the neatest and smartest piece of snake-killing I ever saw was done by my friend Ellis Allen. He was walking with me over our domain one day when, suddenly, right in front of him, a snake raised up its head as if to strike. Without pausing in his stride Allen jumped forward, and as he jumped he kicked at the snake, breaking its back. I don't know that I've ever seen realization, decision, and action in quicker sequence than that.

The Hillsiders went to their work in Bulawayo each day. Most of them had ponies for the journey, and one had a bicycle. My preference was for walking, and I made the distance into town in the morning and back at night on foot.

One evening I was returning home in the half-dark. The road, of course, ran through the veldt. I had a heavy sjambok, a sort of riding-whip made from hippopotamus hide, which had been given me by Charlie Maton and which was seldom out of my hand. Suddenly some animal burst from the bush on the roadside and charged straight at me. I thought it was a lion. I could do nothing but stand still. Instinctively I lifted the sjambok to defend myself, and when the beast was within a yard of me I brought the whip down with all my strength on its head. The brute grunted and swerved past me. The fact that it was on the run created in me the impulse to run after it, and this I did. I caught up with it and began to lay into it with the sjambok, getting a knock or two back. The nature of the battle more than anything else informed me that it was no lion I was fighting, but an ant bear. The combat endured for about fifteen minutes, when the bear gave up. He lay down and, as I thought, died. By this time it was pitch dark.

In the fight we had crossed and recrossed the road and got into the bush. I paced back to the road from the place where the body lay, and marked the spot with a stone on the roadside. Then, after I had had my dinner, I rousted out the members of my half-section in the Troop and, with a lantern to light the way, we went to bring in the corpse. But the carcass had vanished. Next morning, however, we found it some distance from the spot I had marked, and decided to bring it home on our return that evening. Unfortunately, it rained heavily that day, and the rain was followed by hot sunshine. By evening the carcass had reached a state which made the nose a sure guide to its position, so we left it where it was.

For several days after that the ant-bear portion of the road smelled to heaven, and the remarks made by passers-by were sulphurous. But in the end the ants the bear so often had made a meal of made a meal of him. Poetic justice removed the offence.

In the rainy season the road to Hillside became a succession of puddles of mud and water, and top-boots were the only footwear for the pedestrian. Not far from

74

A SWIMMING-POOL NEAR BULAWAYO

74

the town the Matjumschlope river, in the dry season a trickle at most, had to be crossed. One evening, after a day of rain, I reached the river on my way home to find it in such a spate that I hesitated a long while before venturing across. The water was coming down at terrific speed, and rising rapidly. But venture I did at the last and got across in water up to my thighs. That same evening, not much more than half an hour later, a Cape cart with a span of four mules which attempted the crossing was swept downstream, so heavy and so deep had the current become in that space of time. The driver and all the mules were drowned. I think that evening my luck must surely have been in.

Sunday was the day of the week for us of the Hillside coterie. About half a mile from the settlement there was a dam, a beautiful lake surrounded by kopjes and set in magnificent scenery, and we made it our week-end haunt. There was good fishing in the dam, and a native kraal that stood near by gave opportunity for learning of native life and studying Kaffir. I took many photographs here of native scenes and activities.

Below the dam a rocky hollow held a natural pool, which was fine for swimming. This was an attraction which drew lots of people from Bulawayo on fine days.

Of course, when conditions of light or weather made activity out of doors less attractive, we found amusement in Bulawayo. Now and again I would stop in town for the night, when the programme was dinner at the Club, with billiards or poker afterwards, and a ' dossdown ' beside my pal O'Connor. Poker was the most favoured game at the Club, and at times play was high.

75

One night I sat into a game with three friends, and in two hours had won two hundred pounds. I hated the idea of winning so heavily from friends, especially in a school of that size. We played all night, and I did my best to lose. I bet when I was holding no hands worth talking about, and contrived to finish up a winner to the extent only of thirty pounds. If I had played the usual game I would have been a very heavy winner.

I had a dog at this time, a splendid little wirehaired terrier whose name was 'Boy.' He was a real pal. He would walk into town with me faithfully every day. One evening, the rain coming down heavily, I left business at the usual time and expected 'Boy' to keep as usual to my heels. But for some reason that I could not fathom he refused to follow me. I tried every persuasion to the point of becoming annoyed with him, and then it dawned on me that the little fellow was sick. He could do nothing but look at me, whining. I picked him up and carried him the three mile odd home, and next day took him to the vet. 'Boy' had jaundice, and he died of it some days later. The loss of my little friend saddened me for a long time.

CHAPTER VI
CONTACTS WITH CECIL RHODES

IN 1901 Cecil Rhodes came on one of the visits he made periodically to the capital of the state that bore his name. While he was in Bulawayo he laid the foundation-stone of the new Drill Hall.

There was, of course, a large number of camera-men at the ceremony, and I naturally was among them. Rhodes made us rather angry, because after the ceremony he steadfastly denied us any opportunity for getting more than pictures of his back. I can't speak for the others, but for myself his tactics put me on my mettle. I made up my mind to get a good picture of him by hook or by crook, so when he left the platform I unobtrusively followed him.

For a long time I was cheated of any chance by the crowd which eddied round him, but I waited patiently. With the thinning of the crowd opportunity came, and I manœuvred to snatch it. But—bad luck to it!—just when I had him in a good position for snapping he spotted me. Deliberately he walked right up to the camera, spoiling all chance of a picture, and making me hot about the neck.

Nevertheless, I made a pretence at being unconcerned and affected interest in the scenery around. Having, as it were, taken my fill of the beauties of Nature, I then walked casually away for the distance of a yard or two. But through my pretended nonchalance I was keenly aware that he had his eye upon me. The eye of Cecil Rhodes was an eagle eye, and its glance did not make for ease in the person upon whom it was directed. Still, I was not giving up, and when another favourable opportunity seemed to present itself, once again I got the camera into shooting position. Bad luck to it! This time also I was cheated, and Rhodes's look as he closed with me made me feel like curling up.

This second move, however, had brought us close to the ropes that encircled the enclosure. I repeated the scenery-viewing performance, but rather more vacantly, then took a chance to slip under the rope that separated me from the great man, and sat myself on a chair near by. But even then I only had a back view of my intended victim. Still, I considered, a sense of dignity would forbid him attempting to escape by getting over the rope, and my chance would certainly arrive.

It did. I had not been waiting long when Rhodes turned sideways and glanced round the corner of his eye —I imagine to see if I still was on his track. *Click!* I had got him at last—and, *click!*—I had the Administrator into the bargain! You may be sure that I returned home that day with a gratifying sense of achievement.

Two days later I was introduced to Rhodes, an honour which I value to this day. He had the liveliest interest in the youngsters who came to Rhodesia, and I chatted with him for a long time—or, perhaps it would be more correct to say, he chatted with me. He asked me to have some champagne with him, but it happened that just the day previously I had made a bet that I would be teetotal for six months, and I had to refuse.

78

The refusal did not thwart his hospitality, for he offered me a cigar instead, and that I accepted.

In 1902 Cecil Rhodes died at a tiny cottage by the side of a great mansion that was being built for him at Muizenburg, and his body, after lying in state at Cape Town and other centres, was brought to Bulawayo before beginning the final stage of its almost royal progress to the tomb on the high ledge in the Matoppos which he himself had selected.

A special train carried his remains to Bulawayo, and here they were met by the B.S.A. Police and the most prominent men of the town. The coffin was placed on a gun-carriage and was covered by the flag which had meant so much to Rhodes—the Union Jack. Then the cortège moved off to the yet unfinished Drill Hall, the foundation-stone for which he had laid only a short time previously.

The body lay in state in the Drill Hall under a canopy, with four men of the B.S.A. Police to guard it night and day, one man at each corner. The coffin was buried beneath a great mass of wreaths and flowers spreading far beyond the catafalque itself, and all the inhabitants of Bulawayo and from the country for miles around filed past it to do homage to the great Anglo-African. The strain of standing motionless with heads bowed and leaning on the butts of the reversed rifles proved too much for some of the guards. Kipling's story of the Ghurkas watching the feet passing by the royal catafalque may be remembered. Four unbroken hours is too long a spell for men on such duty, and more than one of the guards by the coffin of Rhodes fainted under the strain.

On the day before the interment, trek was made to the Matoppos from all directions. The tracks were black with moving people: men walking, men on horseback, wagons, Cape carts, Scotch carts, vehicles of all sorts and conditions.

The coffin was carried out to the Matoppos that day, and it rested for the night in the dining-room of the series of huts which Rhodes had built, and to which it had been his habit to retire when he needed rest from the pressure of the affairs of the world. The outspan that night was most picturesque, with the camp fires glowing all round under the hills and among the out-spanned wagons. Oxen, tied to the trek chains, stood or lay all about, with knee-haltered horses in great number. The people wandered from camp to camp, falling over oxen in the dark or tripping over tent-ropes. Tents were, however, of small number in proportion to the vast concourse of people, the majority of whom were content to ' doss-down ' in the open. A cordon of police was placed about the outspan to prevent entry to the huts in which rested the body of Rhodes.

My professional longings had not been satisfied by the flashlight photograph which I had taken of the lying-in-state at the Drill Hall. I wanted very badly to secure another of the coffin as it lay in the homelier setting of the huts. I tried for a long time without success to get through the cordon of police, but towards midnight did contrive, by crawling, to manœuvre through the lines. I actually reached the huts, but, to my disappointment after all my efforts, failed to secure the photograph I wanted so badly.

Early in the morning I was at the kopje, where a

80

CECIL RHODES BY THE SITE OF HIS GRAVE IN THE MATOPPOS

platform had been erected for the convenience of a few professional photographers. At the appointed hour the funeral procession came winding up the hill. Troops lined the route, and the coffin on the gun-carriage was followed by the clergy in white surplices. Then came the escort troops with their arms reversed, and the band playing the Dead March. The poignant strains, sad, yet reminding us of offered hope, echoed in the hills about the kopje, round which were massed natives in their thousands, come to pay last tributes to the Great White Chief.

The coffin was lowered into its granite bed as the last offices for the dead were recited.

Now the native Indunas, or chiefs, ascended the kopje to the graveside and gave, one by one, the Royal Salute. Their deep, rich voices sounded afar. They finished, and the thousands of Matabeles about the kopje with single tongue raised their moving valediction to the departed chief. The sound echoed and died away, and so ended a ceremony that must surely remain deeply impressed in the heart and memory of all who witnessed it.

It is not for me to bear witness to the greatness of Rhodes, or to speak of the work he did. His achievement lies open, best witness to the sweep of his soaring mind. His grave in the lonely Matoppos is covered by a simple slab of granite and bears the inscription: " Here lie the remains of Cecil John Rhodes."

The death of Cecil Rhodes was destined to affect my future.

With other members of the firm employing me, I had

taken over a hundred photographs of the last journey to the Matoppos, from the time of the arrival of the coffin at Bulawayo till the carrying out of the last rites at ' World's View.'

In the weeks following the funeral there was a huge demand for our photographs, and work went on at high pressure. I was, myself, turning out hundreds of prints. They had to be exposed during the day, toned and fixed during the late afternoon, then they had to be washed. During the evening they had to be squeegeed on slabs of glass to dry out with the glazed surface then required—a process demanding some hours.

It will be remembered that I was living about three and a half miles out of the town. With the rush of work I was unable to get home at night; I had to take my meals at the Club and I slept on the floor of my dark-room. In the evening one of the partners would come and give me a helping hand, and we seldom got through our work before one or two in the morning. But the rush meant money to the firm, and big money, for prices were high in Bulawayo in those early days.

" Percy," said this partner one night, " you are putting in a lot of overtime. I am going to pay you for it."

" Well," I replied, " I haven't asked you to. I am perfectly willing to work. At the same time, I am paying half the mess bills at Hillside and paying for my meals at the Club as well."

Needless to say, I was grateful for his offer, and glad to accept it.

Just before the end of the month, however, this partner went off to England on vacation. I continued to work late into the night, with an interval of two hours for dinner, when I would perhaps have a game of billiards or poker by way of relaxation. At the end of the month I received my cheque, but there was no sign of the substantial addition to my salary which had been promised. I was not backward in drawing the attention of the office to the matter, and suggested that the omission should be made good. I was told that the matter would be considered.

A week passed, but there was no sign of that additional cheque. The rush of work was still keeping me busy into the early hours of the morning, and there was no indication that the rush was likely to let up. I could get home only from Saturday night until Monday morning. I went to my boss and asked him what he was going to do about overtime. He said that he could not see his way clear to pay me for it.

" Very well," I said, " then I can't see my way clear to work overtime."

So at five o'clock I put on my coat, said " Good night ! " and walked out of the place. There were still a few hundred photographs to go on the slab, and it was essential that they should be taken out of the wash, otherwise they would become too soft to slab, in which event they would be a dead loss.

That night I dined at the Club, and after the meal I sat down for a quiet game of poker. John, as I shall call the boss, also sat into the game. About nine o'clock he got up from his chair.

" Well," he said, " I have some work to do. Sorry, but I must leave you."

He lingered, however, for several minutes, looking at

me hopefully in the expectation that I would join him. There was nothing doing that way, so he went off alone. The work occupied him much longer than it would have occupied me, and he must have found it very tedious.

Each night I left him to it and went home, and he was at it every night till the end of the month. By then John was " fed up to the back teeth." At the end of the month I received my usual cheque, my salary, neither more nor less. And then John sought me out.

" Percy," said he, " I shall have to give you three months' notice."

This was dismissal on terms of our agreement.

" Why? " I asked.

" Well, for one thing, because the photographic department isn't paying."

" That be blowed for a yarn! " said I. " Look at the work we've been turning out for the last two months! Anything else? "

" Well—there have been several complaints lately."

" What sort of complaints? "

" Work not delivered," said he.

" Specify! " I urged him.

" Oh, Mr H—— of Capetown for one. I have a letter from him saying the photos he ordered haven't been forwarded."

" Any others? "

" I can't think of any at the moment," he replied.

On that I turned up my order book and showed him his own receipt for Mr H——'s prints handed him a fortnight previously, then went into the store and found the photographs stuck behind some bottles on a shelf.

What with this faked complaint and the thought of

the broken promise about overtime, I allowed myself to become sarcastic. John told me not to be nasty, and asked me to go and have a drink with him—the usual way of patching up things in those days. I told him bluntly that I didn't want his drink.

" Don't be so costive! " he urged. " Come along, man! "

At last I yielded—to the extent of letting him treat me. I stung him for a large Dry Monopole and a half-crown cigar.

It no sooner became known that I was leaving the firm than I was approached by the manager of Lennons, the biggest firm of chemists in South Africa, who invited me to open a photographic department in their Bulawayo Branch at an increase of £5 a month above the salary I had been getting. But I'd had enough of working for other people. I recalled the advice given by a friend when I was leaving England. " My boy," he said, " don't work for somebody else all your life." It seemed to me that the time had come to play for my own hand and I refused Lennons' offer.

My determination included a resolve to see something more of the country of my adoption. I thought the matter out, and decided to travel down to the Gwanda district, south of Bulawayo. The trouble was, however, that I had not been at all provident since I had arrived in Bulawayo; in fact, I hadn't saved a bean.

Ready money was essential, and the only assets convertible that I had were the articles of furniture I owned in the house at Hillside. These were three and a half miles out of town, and the immediate problem was to find transport to carry them to the Saturday morning sale at the market. Mr Haddon of Messrs Haddon and Sly jumped to my mind. I was well acquainted with him, for we very often lunched in company at the Club on week-days. I went to see him.

" Mr Haddon," I said, " I am leaving Bulawayo to go on the wallaby. I have some furniture at Hillside that I want to get in for the Saturday morning sale. Would you mind lending me a wagon? "

" Certainly, Mr Clark," was the prompt reply. " When would you want it? "

" Saturday morning at 6.30, if it can be managed."

" It will be there, Mr Clark."

I wasn't finished with him at that. I needed provision for the journey.

" Another thing, Mr Haddon," I went on. " I wonder if you would let me have some skoff for the road? I owe you a few pounds as it is; then, I'm chancing my arm on this venture, so you may never be paid."

The warning disturbed him not a whit. He merely asked what amount of stuff I would need. I told him ten pounds' worth would be enough to start with, and he agreed to let me have it.

This incident illustrates the spirit that animated the traders of Rhodesia in those early days. Haddon was one of the best, and he was as good as his word in every way.

On the Saturday morning the wagon arrived to time and the furniture was loaded and conveyed to the morning market. I knew the market master, and, moreover, O'Connor was clerk there. In the ordinary way, articles such as mine were sold more or less in the lump, but these two friends worked it that my pieces were put up separately, and by this arrangement they fetched much better prices.

My next move was to see Mr Bickle, the manager of Lennons who had offered me the new job. I explained my plan to go on trek about the country, taking photographs, and asked him to give me sufficient material on credit to make a start. I gave him the same warning as I had given Haddon, but he was just as ready to trust me as Mr Haddon had been, and agreed to let me have all I wanted. I ran up a bill for about twenty pounds' worth.

Now, it may seem that twenty pounds' worth of photographic material was not a lot to start a business on, but actually there was a good amount of possible cash in a dozen sheets of printing paper. Out in the wilds in the mining districts, a hundred miles from the railway, big profits could be made. For a dozen portrait prints I could get five pounds, and three pounds for half a dozen.

With the money obtained from the sale of my furniture I had a portable canvas studio made, with a changing bag for plates; I also bought a gun and ammunition.

Before setting out I went to see a Major Heany, who had big mining interests. He gave me a commission to take a series of photographs in the group of mines he owned in the Gwanda district.

The regular means of transport was by wagon, and I had not chosen a very good time for starting. An outbreak of Redwater fever was running through the cattle, killing them off by hundreds, and wiping out whole spans of wagon bullocks on trek. There was a great traffic between the rail and the mines, each transport driver vying with the other in the speed with which he could carry goods from one place to another. But, with the outbreak of disease, many now found it impossible to reach their objectives, and numerous wagons were being abandoned on the veldt. This naturally added greatly to the cost of transport.

At last, however, I managed to arrange for the conveyance of myself and my goods at a reasonable price. Everything I needed—or at least everything that I couldn't do without—was packed on the wagon and I set out into the wilds.

CHAPTER VII

ON TREK

THERE is about a long trek by wagon in Africa a fascination difficult to imagine and almost as hard to describe. The freedom of the life, its unconventionality, the constantly changing scene, all combine to create a deep appeal to the lover of outdoors.

One day the route will be through a rich farming country; on the next it will be through a wild expanse of bush. Or, again, the journey will conduct the traveller through ranges of kopjes and along steep drifts. Each shift of scene has its own charm.

With the ox-wagon, travelling is mostly done at night. The inspan is made round about six in the evening and the oxen travel till eleven at the rate of about two miles an hour. They are then outspanned and tied to the trek chain, and the travellers get some sleep. At three in the morning they are again inspanned and the journey is resumed until six. For the next twelve hours the cattle graze at freedom and rest as they will, a proceeding which the humans follow in their human way.

The man with whom I had bargained for transport, Ben, had five wagons. Each had a team of sixteen to eighteen oxen, sufficient to draw them easily under ordinary circumstances. But, owing to the prevailing disease, all the cattle were weak and many of them were sick. The Dutchman in charge drove them hard in order to get his loads delivered before the cattle became unfit for work. Each of the oxen had a name, and some of the names were extraordinary. The teams I travelled with on this journey each had an ' Englishman ' in them, and the beast so named seemed always to get the roughest usage. It was just after the Boer war, and ' Englishman ' in each case got more than his share of the Dutchman's whip, a long-handled affair with a thirty-feet lash.

For the first couple of days on the trek we had heavy rains; on the third morning we outspanned at seven and the cattle were sent out to graze in the care of a couple of native boys. The boys ran across a Kaffir kraal, and the Kaffir beer they got in it was too much for them. They let the cattle stray, and all the seventy-four head of them got lost, so there was no inspanning that evening. What the Dutchman did to the herd-boys when they returned to report their neglect I will not disclose; the Boers had a way of dealing with careless natives which found no favour with the missionaries.

Next morning the Dutchman went in search of the cattle in a downpour of rain. His search lasted three days, on each of which he tramped twenty to thirty miles in the deluge, and in the end he had found only seventy-two of the beasts. The remaining two had to be abandoned; it was probable that they had died of Red-water.

One night during his search he had come back fagged out. Before turning in, we were sitting under the wagon drinking coffee laced with Cape ' Smoke,' as the brandy was called, to counteract the effects of the wet. I gave the Dutchman, or tried to give him, an idea of what London was like. I described the sights, the crowds of people, and miles and miles of streets. Finally, I spoke of the traffic at the Mansion House.

The Dutchman listened to my description in silence, and when I finished made his only comment: " My Gawd! I wouldn't like to look for cattle in *that* place! "

Not long after we had left Bulawayo we met a man riding hard for town. The evening previously, he told us, lions had been prowling around his wagon, and he had wounded one. It was close on sundown, and he tracked the wounded animal to some long grass. He was too wise to follow it into the grass, but next morning he went back to the place and discovered that the lion was still there. Even in daylight it would have been the height of folly to venture among grass standing eight to ten feet high, and in order to drive the lion out he set fire to the grass. He had no sooner done this than the wind changed direction, and he found himself in the path of a real veldt fire. With anything of a wind, a veldt fire travels with bewildering rapidity, and our friend had only one avenue of escape. All he could do was to climb a tree ; fortunately this served him in good stead, but he did not get off without some severe burns.

We were soon to have another warning of lions, for when we got to Sinde Kopjes, some nights later, and while the wagon just preceding us was outspanning, a lion came right up to it and got one of the oxen. All that night we were on the alert, but there was no further sign of Leo. I take it that a ration of one ox per night was enough for him, and that he had not brought his pals.

One of our wagons contained a load of dynamite for the Blanket Mine, and in the Blanket Drift this wagon got stuck in the river bed. It was a day of fearful heat and the dynamite began to melt and run down the side of the wagon. Eventually, with a double span of oxen, thirty-two in number, we managed to get the vehicle free, but there was an outcrop of rock, and the wagon barged into this with a terrible thud, to take a tilt which made it seem that the slightest further pull would bring it over. With the dynamite in that condition, I feared the worst. I reminded myself that I was merely a passenger, and betook myself into the veldt with celerity to await developments behind some rocks.

After a few minutes I heard my Dutch friend calling to me to lend him a hand. I could not refuse, but, believe me, I was in a fearful funk until the wagon was pulled clear.

The first place I set up my tent, so to put it, was at Manzinyama, a hundred miles or so out of Bulawayo on the way to Geelong. There were two stores in the township, and each had a bar. There was also a gaol and a police camp, and the headquarters of a Native Commissioner.

Both of the stores were run by Jews. One of these, Aaron, I found to be a very decent fellow, and from him I hired a hut constructed of *dagga*—that is, ant-heap mixed with cowdung. The hut was to be my headquarters, and outside it I put up my studio.

My first patient was the gaoler, and with his order I was five pounds to the good. Other clients rolled up, and I did so well that within a month I was able to pay off my debts to Haddon and Sly and Messrs Lennons.

The gaoler was a great fellow, and a notable per-

CROSSING THE BLANKET DRIFT WITH A DOUBLE SPAN OF THIRTY-TWO OXEN

former on the tin whistle. During the time I was in Manzinyama he had only one prisoner under his charge. This was an old Indian, who was allowed to sit in the sun all day, if there was any sun, without a guard or any precaution against his escape. The old Indian wandered in and out of the gaol just as he fancied. The gaol was merely a hut of corrugated iron; it was maintained locally that all a prisoner need do to escape was get busy with a tin-opener.

There were mines all about the country round the township, and from these the miners would crowd in on the Saturday nights. They were a mad lot. Their most popular haunt was Aaron's bar. Their favourite game, when anyone entered the bar, was to surround him and yank his shirt out of his trousers. Thus disarranged he had to sing a song, and the penalty for failure was a round of drinks. Aaron himself was the most amusing victim of the dodge. Jovial of countenance, it was a sight to see him with his shirt hanging out and his face glowing as he ' obliged ' with a ditty. It is to be added that he never failed to put up the drinks as well.

One day a miner from the Geelong Mine drifted into the store in quest of a drink. He was flush with the earnings of a few months, and he was on his way to Bulawayo to ' blow ' them on what he called a jolly good time. While he was standing at the bar a smart little dog-cart pulled up outside and a short, rather stoutish little man got down from it and came in. His name was Werner, and he was manager of the Geelong hotel and store. He looked the miner over and spotted the roll of blankets on the floor.

" Hullo! " he said, none too pleasantly. " So you

thought you would diddle me out of what you owe me, did you? Better stump up!"

The miner, a fellow of good physique, refused flatly to part.

"All right!" said Werner. "I'll take it out of your hide."

"You!" sneered the miner. "You couldn't punch a dent in a pat of butter."

By this time Werner's coat was off and his sleeves rolled up, and he invited the bigger fellow to step outside. The miner was nothing loath.

It was a right royal battle. What Werner was lacking in weight and size he made up for in quickness and energy. He was in and out like lightning, banging home blows that were full of snap. The bigger fellow certainly landed one or two good ones, but the fight was carried to him from start to finish by Werner, who amply fulfilled his promise to take it out of the miner's hide. It was a treat to see Werner's footwork and the way he could snatch at an opening.

Later on I came to know Werner very well, and always found him a jolly fine fellow. But, then, men who can fight that way usually are good chaps.

While I was in Manzinyama I got a lot of fishing in the Umshibese river. There was a good bathing pool in it close to the town that the police troopers and visitors frequently used.

One afternoon on one of my fishing visits I was making my way round the pool, pushing through some undergrowth under a high bank, when as I shoved a branch aside I came face to face with a snake that was swinging on a bough within a couple of feet of my head.

I jumped back, and as I did so I felt a sharp sting through the seat of my pants. It was, I supposed, the suspended snake's mate. I quickly dispatched the snake in front of me and turned about to find the other, but there was no snake to be seen. " My goodness! " I said to myself. " What on earth shall I do? I can't suck the poison out myself, and there's nobody within half a mile! " Off I started to find help, and as I bolted I clapped my hand on the spot where I had been stung. My fingers closed on a big thorn! I went back to my fishing.

Altogether I was about three weeks in Manzinyama, and in that time I made a profit of seventy-five pounds.

My next move was to Geelong, where the mine was one of the largest in the Gwanda district. It boasted a general manager, a mine manager, and it had a large clerical staff, with many engineers and miners. The large store combined with an hotel and dining-room was owned by the Copthall Stores Company, and, as already mentioned, Werner was the manager.

The management of such a business in such a settlement called for a man of Werner's courage and fistic ability and even temper, because Geelong at that time was the spit of Bret Harte's *Roaring Camp*. Though many of the miners chummed up for messing in groups of five, a good lot of them boarded at the hotel. If the food didn't happen to suit them they would curse the native waiters, and thought nothing of throwing food, plate and all, through a window. But Werner saw to it that they paid for any damage of the sort.

It was in the late afternoon that I arrived in Geelong.

95

After dinner, which I had with the staff in their private dining-room, I was taken round by a man on the clerical staff, whom I knew, to see the sights. We wound up at the men's quarters, into which we were invited for a drink. The room was only about twelve-foot square, and there were about half a dozen men round the bottle. The atmosphere was decidedly foggy, but we had a drink. The men had had a few already, and before long guns were pulled. It was all a lark to the miners, but my education up to that time hadn't given me any taste for fun of that sort, and I discovered that the air on the other side of the door was fresher.

As in all mining towns, gambling was the great diversion, and poker the most favoured game. Men rode in from the neighbouring mines on a Saturday night and sat gambling pretty well right through to Sunday evening, when they rode back to their work. Their week-ends were lively.

I was as keen on poker as anybody, and I found myself attached to a party that made a regular thing of it on Saturday nights. One night, two of us were waiting in the hotel dining-room for the gathering of the school, and to pass the time we started a game between us. While we were playing a stranger rode up, dismounted, and lounged into the room. For a time he looked on, then asked if he might join in. We said he might, and explained our rules. Cash on the table was the first of them, and we had a general penalty of ten bob paid by each of the school to anybody getting four of a kind, and a pound for a straight flush.

My original opponent dealt, and it was up to the stranger to 'ante' with a shilling. I made it two shillings to come in and four to play. The dealer came in and the stranger threw in his hand. Myself and the dealer both raised before the draw. I was holding 2,3,5,6 of clubs, and drew one card. My opponent stood pat. My opponent bet until his cash gave out, and he had to see me. I had filled with the four of clubs for a straight flush. My opponent put down four queens. That, you'll agree, was tough luck on the stranger. He hadn't drawn a card, had lost his ' ante,' and had to cough up thirty bob in penalties. Then his horse went and died on him.

Shooting was indulged in promiscuously. I was in Geelong five weeks and in that time a native was shot by a white man. I myself saw the manager of a neighbouring mine chase the Geelong compound manager over the dumps with a shotgun. Practice in shooting was had on Sundays with bottles as targets. There was, of course, no dearth of targets. The range was a hundred yards, and each competitor contributed a shilling or half a crown to the pool, which went to the highest scorer.

Take it from me that life in the camp was wild and woolly. I had made friends with an underground contractor—call him ' Plinge '—who roomed next door to an out-sized Norwegian. For some reason this Scan. had taken a grudge against Plinge, and had got into the way of waiting for him at night, threatening to shoot him if he went near his room. Plinge, who was a hefty enough fellow himself, happened to be a peaceable sort, not looking for trouble. Rather than bring the matter to a head by going to his own quarters, Plinge ' dossed-down ' with me ; he shared my room for a fortnight.

G

97

One night Plinge and myself had been playing poker with the store-keeper, who also acted as barman, and, our game finished, we went into the bar for a final before getting to bed. The bar had only one door. While we were having our drink the Norwegian came in, and started straight away on Plinge. Plinge backed before him right to the other end of the room.

It was time, I thought, that this bullying came to an end, and I said as much to Plinge in an undertone, urging him to stick up for himself. But my friend backed right to the wall. He then had to take what he got or defend himself. Both the barman and I urged Plinge to go for the Scan., and to go for him quickly, and the barman nipped from behind the counter. He and I pinched the Scan.'s guns while he was bullying Plinge.

At last Plinge went into action, and he and the Norwegian went at it hammer and tongs in a real rough-house. Then the Norwegian hit the floor and stayed there. I told him to get up and stop acting foolishly. He got up.

" Have a drink," I said to him, " and forget it! "

Well, he had a drink, and began to abuse Plinge all over again.

" Go on, Plinge! " said the barman. " Let him have it."

Plinge saw there was no help for it, and went for him, and in the end the Scan. was chucked out of the bar into the night. Though we did not know it, he dropped dead before he had gone three hundred yards. As far as I know, the doctor may have said the Scan. died of short-ness of breath, or something of that sort, but we were troubled by no inquiry. In any case, the fight was a fair one from start to finish ; at all odds the blame for the row lay completely on the Scan. himself.

During my stay in Geelong a miner in a neighbouring mine was sandbagged while returning to his habitation one night. He was stripped of all he had, and that included his month's pay and a gold watch. The footpad was never traced, but the miner got his watch back somehow three years later.

There was also at this time a robbery of Zeederberg's coach, which carried the gold weekly from the mine to Bulawayo. Nobody was killed in the hold-up, but the robbers made a good haul. It was some months before they were caught and convicted.

I had been given the use of two rooms by the mine management, one to sleep in and the other for a studio, and I proceeded to take many photographs of the mine.

I went down one day to secure a flashlight of the workings. The only position from which a good view was possible was from the top of a narrow ledge of rock which had an eight-foot drop front and back. The ledge was so narrow that I had to get a native to hold the tripod legs of the camera to prevent them from slipping over the edges. I got everything nicely prepared for taking a good picture, and let off the flash. It so startled the nigger that he jumped backward and went smack to the foot of the eight-foot drop. The fall hardly hurt him, for the natives are tough, but in going he took the camera legs with him. By the greatest good fortune I managed to save the camera from taking the toss too. It was a narrow squeak, for if it had gone there would have been an end to my business activities for some time.

As a fact, however, my trip was about to be inter-rupted—as you will see. But before I come to that I must get an incident into its proper place. The first act took place in Geelong, and the second in another spot many moons later.

There came into the camp one day three fellows ' on the wallaby ' who were walking from the Transvaal to Rhodesia in search of work. They seemed to be very decent characters, and it happened that I was the first to encounter them. I gave them dinner, let them have a doss-down in my room for the night, and breakfast in the morning. Before they set out again I took them to the store and bought them skoff for the journey. Then I handed them a quid to assist them on their way, and they went off with every appearance of being appre-ciative.

Now comes the sequel. A considerable time later I was travelling north to the Zambesi. After ten days of wagon trek from the railhead I arrived at the Wankie colliery. Very likely I was not an attractive sight in a pair of old khaki slacks and a khaki shirt, and with the thick dust of the road upon me. I wouldn't say that I was any too clean. I was making for the mines office to see if I could fix up some accommodation, when I met with a fellow in an immaculate white suit. He fairly glistened in the sunlight and dazzled the eyes. But with all this marvellous change in his appearance I recog-nized him as one of the three to whom I had played the Samaritan at the Geelong mine in the previous year. Of course, I stopped and greeted him.

" Hullo, old chap! " said I. " You seem to have struck it all right. How's things? "

A FLASHLIGHT PHOTOGRAPH TAKEN IN THE GEELONG MINE

100

He stared me up and down slowly from head to heel.

" Oh, yes! " he drawled. " You are the photographer man I met down in the Gwanda, aren't you? "

It seemed to me that my quid was uppermost in his mind, and that he thought getting it back was uppermost in mine.

" Yes, that's me," I said; and I turned sharply on my heels and pushed off. I ran straight into Mr (now Sir) Bourchier Wrey, who had been, it will be remembered, my troop captain in 1901. He was with Sir Charles Metcalfe.

" Hullo, Clark! Where are you off to? " Mr Wrey hailed me. I told him; he introduced me to Sir Charles, and they invited me to dine with them at the doctor's house, where they were staying.

The fellow in the immaculate whites was also at the dinner-party—pulling corks! He was the doctor's orderly.

The moral of the yarn—" Don't judge by appearances, especially in a new country! "—has, you'll notice, a double edge. It cuts both ways.

I stopped five weeks at the Geelong. In my second month in the Gwanda district I made a profit of a hundred and twenty-five pounds, and I had a hundred pounds' worth of orders waiting for me at another large mine in the district, the West Nicholson.

At the end of that second month, however, an appeal reached me from my friend O'Connor. " For God's sake come back! " it ran. " I am on the bust and can't get off it! "

O'Connor was my friend. The question whether I

would or wouldn't have the influence on him he imagined was unimportant. It was enough for me that he thought I could help him. I left orders and everything and, feeling that wagon travel would be much too slow, took the first coach available back to Bulawayo.

I found O'Connor in a deplorable state. The process of getting him ' off the bust ' involved going on the bust myself. But my debauches were of a minor nature, and I feel no shame for them because they helped in getting my friend back to the condition of his natural splendid self.

CHAPTER VIII

OFF AGAIN

AMONG the people whom I met again on my return to Bulawayo was my former boss, he who had promised me extra payment for my work on the Rhodes funeral photographs. He had got back from his trip to England.

We were chatting together in the Club billiard room after lunch when his partner walked in. I called him over, then turned to the other. " Did you or didn't you promise me overtime for that work on Rhodes' funeral? " I asked him.

" I did," he said promptly.

" Well, I never got it," I told him. " All I got was the sack."

The returned partner looked at the other, then turned to me.

" If I hadn't gone home," he said, " you would be with us now."

" Thanks! " said I. " I'm glad you went home."

The slap was at the fellow who had dismissed me, but it happened to be true. Working for myself I had done well, and I meant to be off once more on my travels as soon as O'Connor was himself again. It was in my mind this time to go east, towards Umtali, following the railway more or less, and striking out into the mining districts. When the time came for moving, O'Connor decided to come with me.

I procured a draft on an Umtali bank, and this I carried with me. I also put a considerable sum of money in a trunk, which I intended to keep forwarding to the various towns we meant to visit *en route*. A further sum I carried with me for running expenses.

We made our first stop at Gwelo, a hundred miles from Bulawayo, and from there we hired a mule cart to carry us to the Bonsor mine. The trip was a short one, but it cost me fourteen pounds. That, as it chanced, was pretty well a dead loss, because the trip was unprofitable. There was a photographer in the town near at hand and he had toured the mines. O'Connor and I got back to the rail by ox-wagon, which was cheaper by a lot.

We went on to Salisbury, sending the trunk with our cash on by goods train. Salisbury then, though a fairly large town, was a tin one—like most of the towns at that period of the country. Where iron was not used, wood was the material, and a brick building was a showplace. O'Connor and myself put up at the Commercial Hotel and began to look for business. There wasn't any —at least, not enough to enable us to pay our way. We decided to move on.

Before we could shift, however, we had our hotel bill to pay. We were out of ready cash, and the trunk had not arrived. We wired to Gwelo, but could get no news of it. It seemed to have been lost. Then a week after our coming to Salisbury we were informed that it had been found and was being sent on. Thereafter we went to meet every train, questioning the officials until they were sick of the sight of us. With each train we got the same answer, " No advice has been received." Then one day, moodily watching a train depart after our usual inquiries and the usual answer, we espied the trunk in the goods van sailing by us on the way to Umtali! I'll describe our feelings mildly and say we were most annoyed.

The only course now was to get after the trunk. We had our railway tickets, fortunately, but no money to meet our hotel bill. I sought the hotel proprietor and explained the situation. It was evident that he had heard a similar story and had been bitten, for his attitude was nothing if not sceptical. I offered him a cheque for the bill, showing him the draft on Umtali. This gave him just enough assurance to let us take our luggage and go.

We got to Umtali, a lovely little town in a beautiful setting, and thought our troubles were over. All I had to do was to collect some money on the draft in order to release my trunk, which had been sent carriage forward. I went to the bank, presented the draft, and asked that an account be opened for me. I was informed that as a preliminary to any business I should have to be identified.

I padded up and down the town's one street, hunting for some one known at the bank who also knew me. I searched every possible place where men might congregate, but without any luck.

There seemed to be no hope. With money at the station and money in the bank, we were homeless and penniless. Then suddenly, in the nadir of despair, I bumped into a man whom I knew very well, but who I had thought was in Bulawayo. I told him my story and begged him to come along to the bank and vouch for me.

" Nothing easier, old chap," said he. " I'm the bank manager! "

He had recently been transferred, and I didn't know anything of it.

The hotel that O'Connor and I put up at, the King's Arms, was run by one of the pioneers of old Umtali, a sturdy woman of middle-age known as ' Mother Brown.' She was as stout of mind as she was strong of body, not at all above handling an uppish customer single-handed and chucking him out neck and crop. But if she was formidable to any that tried to impose on her, she could listen to a hard-luck story with sympathy, and nobody in genuine need went out of her place hungry. I have, myself, seen Mother Brown go well out of her way several times to help down-and-outers. Her neighbours thought a lot of her.

On the ground by the hotel, the day we took up our quarters there, the skins of two lions were pegged out. They had been shot near the hotel on the previous night. Lions were constantly prowling round the town, and the young bloods made a great to-do about going after them. Not, however, with consistent success. Once when lions were reported a couple of the bloods fixed up a platform in a tree near the spot where the brutes were supposed to be. After they had waited for a long time, they did see the movement of a large animal in the bars of moonlight. It came within range and, taking careful aim, they both fired. The monster dropped. Exercising great caution, they let some time elapse before descending. At last it seemed beyond doubt that the brute was dead. They got down and approached it cautiously. It was dead all right. But their lion wasn't quite of the right shape. They had killed a stray donkey!

The next objective for O'Connor and myself was the Penhalonga mine, not very many miles out of Umtali. We had every hope of doing good business there, especially as there was to be a large camp of volunteers out on manœuvres at this time. The Penhalonga was reached by way of the Christmas pass.

We outspanned about midnight in the pass, and my partner and myself were having some coffee before turning into our blankets for two or three hours when a couple of our native wagon-drivers got up a friendly scrap. They laid into each other and called each other all sorts of names in their own language, much to O'Connor's amusement and mine. Then one of the boys called the other, in English, " a bloody nigger."

" What! " exclaimed the other. " *Me* a nigger! Then what are you? "

" Me? "

" Yes, you—what are you? "

" Oh," said the first one, easily, " I'm a Scotchman! "

At Penhalonga we hired a room in a hotel kept by a German. We did good business, and when the troops raised camp we decided to go with them, by wagon, back to Umtali. In checking the bill for our accommodation we found that the landlord was greatly overcharging us. We taxed him with it, and he became abusive. That was not the way to deal with a hot-headed Irishman like O'Connor. O'Connor lost his temper and there was a fight. That being over, we paid the landlord what was really due him, neither more nor less, then packed our stuff and joined the wagon.

O'Connor, still rather sore at the landlord's attempt to swindle us, indulged in a trick somewhat childish but perhaps understandable. He locked the door of our room and took the key away with him, chucking it later at hazard into the veldt. It was only after this had happened that I found I had left my raincoat hanging on the door of the room. I couldn't afford to lose the coat, so telling O'Connor to go on with the wagon, I rather reluctantly dropped off and began walking back to the hotel. But I could see myself in a quandary. I couldn't very well ask the landlord, our parting with him having been strained, to open the door for me, even if he did happen to have a duplicate key. In fact, in order to get into the room I should have to dodge him, and when I got back to the hotel I found this none too easy. Eventually, however, I managed to slip back the catch of the window and recover my coat. But I had to foot it to Umtali.

Back again in Bulawayo my mind was exercised on the question of where I should go next. I was tired of trains and hotels; I longed to get away from beaten tracks. I decided finally to go north, and that with a definite object. I wanted to see the Victoria Falls, and I planned to make a trip which, as far as I know, had never been attempted before. This was to follow the Zambesi from the Falls to the coast. O'Connor meantime had made arrangements to go trading to Barotseland. Our route would be together as far as the Falls, from which O'Connor would travel by the upper Zambesi, while I struck eastward along the lower part of the river.

As a necessary preliminary I went to see Mr Marshall

THE AUTHOR (LEFT) AND O'CONNOR BEFORE LEAVING FOR
THE ZAMBESI

Hole, Civil Commissioner at Bulawayo, who gave me a letter to all the District Commissioners on my intended route, asking them to give me all possible assistance, especially with regard to securing carriers.

O'Connor left ahead of me. He had to fix up trading licences and so forth. In a few weeks' time, when his arrangements would be made, I was to meet him at Wankie colliery, then just opened.

The first part of the journey to Wankie had to be made by construction train, in trucks containing railway material. The trucks were open and abominably dirty. There was nothing to afford protection from the sun, which in the daytime beat down on one cruelly. The railway in its course northward went through very wild country.

I stopped at the railhead for two nights. Lions and other vermin were plentiful about the construction camp there, and most of the workmen took their sleep in the trees, for sleeping on the ground was dangerous. They dossed down on platforms among the branches, well out of reach of marauding lions. The other men slept in *scherms*, otherwise known as ' scarems '—that is, in tents hedged about high with poles and thorn bushes.

Transport from railhead north to Wankie colliery was done by wagon, with a Scotch cart to carry the mails. I made arrangements with a transport rider for the conveyance of myself and my goods to Wankie. The transport rider was colonial born, with a fine knack of handling both oxen and natives. The trip occupied ten days, but I enjoyed every minute of it—even its accidents.

The shooting to be got on the route was plentiful and varied. One morning, on going to collect the cattle, we found a sable antelope feeding with them. But it wasn't such lucky hunting to secure it as food for ourselves and the boys; we could get birds or buck for the pot almost any time on the trek.

Sometimes we had to dig in dry river-beds for water, but, generally speaking, there was plenty to be got for the cattle.

After inspanning one night we travelled in the usual way till dawn, when it was discovered that the water-barrel was missing. Owing to negligence on the part of one of the boys it had been left behind at the last out-span. The boy that was culpable got a good hiding from the owner, and was sent back ten miles to retrieve the barrel. He had to do the journey in the heat of the day while the wagon party rested, but he was back at sun-down with the barrel. He showed no resentment over the hiding or the task imposed on him; he knew he was justly served. As a fact, the boss was well liked by the boys, for he looked after them well.

Leaving the wagon one afternoon to go shooting, I lost myself. I still wasn't much good on the veldt, and I hadn't taken a guide with me. Towards sundown I made tracks for the wagon, taking my direction by the sun. The general direction was right enough, but the exact bearing was hard for a novice to find. I walked and walked, getting more and more worried every minute, but hoping to come on the wheel-marks of the wagon. When it seemed that I was never going to find the trail, I fired my rifle, still keeping my line. I kept firing shots, and at last was located by one of the wagon-boys. It turned out that my line was more or less right, but I had gone over the wagon-tracks without noticing them.

There was a lot of rough going on the way to Wankie, but the toughest part of all was at a place called Mica Hill. What road there was degenerated here into a boulder-strewn track. We came on it in the middle of the night. As a passenger I could sit in the wagon all I wanted to, but I had got into the way, when the going was rough, of getting out to walk. But it seemed that I was always getting out to walk, and I finally determined to stick in the wagon however bad the going might be. It happened that I was exercising this determination when we hit Mica Hill.

' Hit ' is the apt word. The jolting was terrific. Time and again I escaped going overboard merely by the skin of my teeth. The boxes loaded in the wagon seemed to have hundreds of corners. With every jolt I found a new one. But I stuck to the wagon. There came a terrific crash, and the wagon stopped.

In the pitch dark I waited for a while, then got down. The disselboom of the wagon—that is, the pole to which the trek chain is attached—had snapped. We were stuck until a new one could be made from a tree. We were pondering the situation when one of the wagons coming up behind had a wheel knocked off.

Have I remembered to say that wagon-travelling is fascinating?

We got to Wankie, as I have said, in ten days. At that time (the beginning of 1903) the mine had just been started. The mine-manager's house was on the point of being completed, and there were only a few huts dotted about on the surrounding kopjes. The fitter's shop was merely a lean-to shelter with a corrugated iron roof, but otherwise open to the winds. The power-house, a building about twenty feet square, was the only place in the camp where one could get a bath, and that was in rather oily water drawn from the engine.

Although the place was in such a rudimentary state there already was a hospital with a doctor and one nurse. This provision was very necessary owing to the unhealthiness of the spot. Most people on the mine went down before long with malaria. Nowadays the scene is completely changed. Where I first saw an open *vlei* there is now a huge congeries of buildings: furnaces, power-houses, shops. And the place has been made healthy. In my first visit the place was infested with lions, three being shot right in the camp.

My first concern on arriving at Wankie was to find accommodation. The mine office had none to give me. Wandering round, I came on a fellow who had just set up a butchery. He had only one hut, serving him for all purposes, but he made me welcome and offered me part of the floor for my bed. Though sleeping in the open would have been no hardship, I accepted the offer.

One morning in this hut I awoke to find a snake by my blankets. To this day I am scared of snakes and hate them like poison—then I probably felt this revulsion more acutely. On a sudden movement my visitor slid into a hole between my bed and the wall. Well, whenever I saw a snake I could not rest content until that snake was a corpse, and I knew there would be neither

SABLE ANTELOPE SHOT ON THE ROAD TO WANKIE

rest nor sleep for me until this particular snake was obliterated. I procured a stick and sat myself down to watch the hole, motionless. I waited quite a couple of hours before his sliminess appeared. After a cautious survey of the hut he slid into the open. One cut with the stick and he was done for. I tell you, I hate snakes.

I made a round of visits in the camp and got to know all the miners in their quaintly-named habitations. There was ' Starvation Kopje,' ' The Workhouse,' ' The Castle,' and I can't remember what. They were all huts of the *dagga* and pole make of walls, with thatched roofs—a mode of construction giving huts that are cool to live in.

The mine-manager's house reached completion during my stay, and with three others, mine officials, I was invited to the house-warming. After the common diet of road and camp the dinner was splendid, and we all had a marvellous time, keeping it up well into the morning. I took a flashlight of the party.

A Native Commissioner, Andrew Dale by name, occupied a house of the pole and *dagga* type on a neighbouring kopje. It was to him that I went for carriers for my journey to the Falls, and I found him the best of fellows, though a fortnight went by before he managed to collect and persuade eighteen natives to accompany me. The intended route was through bad country, much infested by lions. Besides that, there was fear of the tribe about the Falls, the Barotse, who were deadly enemies of the Matabele.

Andrew Dale's district was a large one, but very sparsely populated. The natives trusted him and came

H   113

to him with their troubles. It was his custom to visit the Zambesi every second or third month; he did the journey on horseback, and habitually made his camp on a kopje only two miles from the Victoria Falls. I have immortalized him by naming the kopje on which he used to camp ' Dale's Kopje.' I met Dale after the Great War—in which he was permanently lamed—and I told him what I had done. He was greatly bucked about it.

Anyone who comes to see the Falls will find a visit to Dale's Kopje well worth while. It gives a really magnificent view of the Zambesi, with its beautiful stretches of lakelike water and its islands studded with palms.

To return, however, to Wankie. Another step towards its urbanization was effected before I left by the arrival on horseback of a troop of seven of the B.S.A. Police to establish the police camp.

From my inquiries I learned that I had not realized the nature of the difficulties that I should have to overcome in my proposed journey along the course of the Zambesi to the coast.

The course of the river for forty-five miles through the gorge below the Falls was almost impracticable. Two or three years after I first visited Wankie the District Commissioner at Livingstone and Professor Lamplough did negotiate this forty-five miles, but, although they had a large number of natives with them, the trip took them three weeks.

Much to my disappointment I abandoned my plans and decided to travel up the Zambesi to the interior. O'Connor joined me and with our native bearers we started out for the river. I should be ungrateful if I neglected to mention another companion. This was a wirehaired terrier pup, a bitch, that I acquired in Wankie. She became my great friend, and she would have been an asset to any party. I shall say more about her later.

CHAPTER IX

FIRST SAFARI

THERE are people who, having lived a few years in Africa, flatter themselves that they know the native and all his idiosyncrasies. The pioneers would never make such a claim. If questioned on the subject they would confess that the native is harder to understand than a woman. They might put it this way: that the more you know the native the less you know of him, and that the more you think of him the less you think of him.

My first real experience of the natives was got on the trip to Victoria Falls, when I had eighteen of them as carriers. My chief feeling about these boys was one of annoyance. Half of them were quick goers, and the other half were absolute snails. If I went ahead with the quick ones, the slow ones would lag behind. This lagging gave them a chance to plant select portions of my goods off the road for collection on their return journey.

A great deal of my trouble, of course, was due to inexperience. My goods, for example, were not packed in the proper way, and the peculation by my carriers resulted in odd shortages. Four hundred miles above the Falls I found myself completely out of baking-powder. But here again I could put the loss down to my education account since I discovered the 'yeasty' usefulness of Kaffir beer in making bread. It makes quite good

MY CARRIERS

bread, as a matter of fact. So, I found, would Eno's Fruit Salts—though it is too expensive a substitute for baking-powder.

The trip of just over a hundred miles from Wankie to Victoria Falls took us over a week. Though there was a road of sorts, we were able—having a guide—to make use of kaffir paths as short cuts. Much of our travelling was done by moonlight, and we got along quicker and easier in the coolness of the night than we might in the heat of the day. It was exceedingly rough going between Wankie and Matetsi, but we put in about twenty miles per day on the trek of eight days. The motor-road between Wankie and the Falls nowadays covers 113 miles. In our wanderings, that first safari, we must have covered a good deal more than that.

The country, particularly about Matetsi, was lion-infested. Years later, when a farm was taken up at Matetsi, the farmer shot over a hundred lions on the farm itself inside a period of three years. On our trek we had, as may be imagined, many a lion scare.

One night we were marching along the dry bed of the Matetsi river. Half the carriers were with O'Connor and myself, and the other half—as usual—were about half a mile behind. Suddenly the carriers with us dropped their loads and huddled into a bunch.

" What's the matter? " we demanded.

" Lion, baas—lion! "

Sure enough we could hear something moving in the reeds of the river bank.

" Get on, you fools! " we ordered, and hustled them into activity.

About half a mile farther on we outspanned, and

waited for the rest of the carriers to turn up. Half an hour passed without a sign of them.

"Bud," I said to O'Connor, "we'll have to go back and bring them in."

"Nothing doing," said he. "I haven't lost any lions and I'm looking for none."

"But the boys have our stuff."

. "Can't help that," he replied. "Stuff or no stuff, I'm not going."

There was a Matabele boy in our outfit whose ambition in life was to shoot something, but who had never handled a gun in his life. I handed this fellow a shotgun, and we set off together back along the trail. We found the missing carriers huddled together at the spot where the advance party had taken fright. I got them on the move, then turned to the Matabele boy.

"Now, Tom," said I, "you go and shoot that lion."

And sure enough, so bucked was he at having a gun to pop off at last, he went straight into the reeds.

"Come back, you fool!" I yelled. "Come back!"

Back he came, but started picking up stones from the river bed and chucking them at the lion. I didn't wait.

That night we had a dozen fires going in a ring, and O'Connor and myself slept in the centre. Lions surrounded us, but the fires and the boys in watches kept them off. I said Matetsi was 'lion-infested.' That is putting it mildly.

Part of our journey lay through the Katuna valley. This is a long, waterless stretch of very wild country, which, if I remember rightly, Livingstone called "The Valley of Death." Here we had no water for two days.

We dug in all the likeliest places, but found no drop of moisture. Then we discovered what thirst meant. One may go hungry for a long time, but to go thirsty is quite another thing. Our tongues dried up and swelled, but we plugged along doggedly. One and another of our carriers fell out exhausted, but we managed to get them going with brandy from our small stock.

We were getting out of the 'Valley of Death' at long last, and were rejoicing in the knowledge that we could not be far from water, when on the horizon a welcome sight appeared. This was a Scotch cart drawn by four oxen. A native was driving, and by his side was an enormous figure of a man—a Jew trader trekking south. To us he was an angel in disguise.

The cart halted, and greetings were exchanged. I fear, however, that they were perfunctory on our part. Our gaze was fixed on two large water-sacks that hung on the cart. They were of the canvas kind which, by evaporation, keeps water marvellously cool.

" A drink? " the angel suggested.

" Please," we said modestly.

" Whisky or gin? "

" I don't give a damn," said I, " but, if anything, a drop of gin."

The gargantuan Hebrew angel brought out a *comiche* of proportions worthy of his own remarkable bulk, and started pouring gin into his huge enamel mug. I said " When! " very quickly to the gin, but so delayed ' whenning ' to the water that followed that the Jew's eyes began to pop. " Enough? " he asked. " Not yet," said I, and I waited until he had poured out a good pint. I can't believe that nectar itself could have tasted better than that drink did to me. I took it off slowly to the last drop. " Another?" the angel invited. " Yes, please," I replied. " But without the gin this time."

O'Connor was ministered to in the same way, and the carriers were given a ration from the cask that was carried under the cart. And so, after blessing our Trans-jordanic and bulky friend, and giving him the down-country news, we went on our way.

On the Matetsi river, some thirty miles from the Victoria Falls, we halted for a day to give our çarriers a rest. From that distance we could see the spray of the Falls, for it often rises to a height of over three thousand feet. But though our Jordan thus was in sight, we had considerably farther than the crow-flight of thirty miles to cover before we reached it. The last part of our trek was harder going than any of it. We were in very tough country indeed. The night following our rest our camp was sixteen miles from the Falls, and the roar of them filled our ears.

The sixteen-mile march next day was notably strenuous. It was eleven at night before we made camp under a great baobab (the cream of tartar tree) about a mile from the Victoria Falls. The night was brilliant with moonlight, and it was the time of full flood on the river. Tired though I was I could not let the need of rest come between me and my first sight of the mighty cataract.

I shall never forget my first sight of the Victoria Falls; there is nothing in all my experiences so deeply im-pressed on my memory. My first view was from the western end, whence I looked over the Devil's cataract

WATER-HOLES IN THE VELDT

right along the chasm. It was like entering some wonderful cathedral. In the foreground was the magnificent bluff of Barouka island with the tumbling waters of the cataract. Beyond, veiled in spray, the main fall could be glimpsed as it leapt, roaring, into the chasm four hundred feet below. The rain forest, shadowy and ghostly, wreathed and changed before the Falls, delighting the eye with moving shapes, and the lunar rainbow, pale and shimmering, gave the whole scene a touch of faery. Awed beyond telling, I felt as if I stood in the presence of some majestic Power quite ineffable. My hat came off, and for an hour I stood bareheaded, lost in rapture.

No. I shall never forget my first view of the Falls, full in flood and drenched in moonlight. Since that first hour I have seen the Falls a thousand times by day and night, but I never tire of seeing them. The fascination dwells. I am drawn to them time and time again, never disappointed of a new picture, a new phase of beauty. On my return after journeys down country I often would find myself soaked by the thick mist in the rain forest on a visit to the Falls. I would go home and change, then take another stroll down to the Devil's cataract. Then, before I realized what I was doing, I would be half-way through the rain forest and drenched a second time. After spending thirty-two years within a mile of the spot where I first saw the Falls by moonlight, it is still my favourite view.

The Victoria Falls were discovered by David Livingstone, the missionary-explorer, in November 1855. The natives call them *Mose-oa-tunya*, ' The Smoke that Thunders.' How appropriate the name is will be gathered from the facts I have already mentioned—that the spray can be seen from thirty miles off, and the roar of the waters heard from sixteen miles away. The width of the Falls from east to west is one and a quarter miles, and the waters drop, as I have said, into an immense chasm four hundred feet deep. The chasm narrows to an outlet about a quarter of a mile from the western end of the Falls, and through this outlet the whole volume of the river races at terrific speed to pass in succession spots in the gorge with the descriptive and suggestive names of ' the Boiling Pot,' ' Knife-Edge,' ' Danger Point.' The gorge, over which is thrown the Zambesi bridge, zigzags curiously for some miles below the Falls, and extends forty-five miles in all.

I recorded my arrival at the Falls the following morning by carving my name on the baobab tree, and the date —May 8, 1903. After this feat—not very like myself, but perhaps excusable in the circumstances—we set out for the ' Old Drift,' five miles above the Falls.

The Old Drift was the port of entry, as it were, into North-western Rhodesia. I have never been able to ascertain where it got the name from. The Zambesi at this point is at its deepest and narrowest for hundreds of miles above the Falls.

Here we had to part with our carriers. They were Matabele, and nothing would induce them to cross the river, for on the other side were the Barotse, their deadly enemies, who, they said, would kill them. We paid them off, and they lost no time in starting on their return journey to Wankie. They were probably in a hurry to pick up what they had planted of mine on the road up. I take note of their fear of crossing the river because months later, when I tried to persuade Barotse carriers to cross with me on the journey south, they refused in turn on the ground that the Matabele would kill them.

At the Old Drift, however, we had to get to the other side of the river. For two hours we sat on the southern bank of the Zambesi popping off a rifle at intervals to attract attention. At long last we saw a native dug-out set out from the opposite shore. It was paddled such a distance directly up-river that we began to wonder if it was coming for us at all. The reason for the manœuvre, of course, lay in the strength of the current, as we presently saw. It wanted a very long slant indeed from the other bank to bring the dug-out precisely to the spot where we were waiting for it. Several such voyages were needed to bring our goods after us to the northern bank. At this time there were no other sorts of craft on the river save such dug-outs, the native boats made by the hollowing-out of tree trunks. Canadian canoes, tubs, and launches began to appear at a later date.

Dug-outs are ticklish things to handle, but the Barotse are excellent river-boys. Standing to their work, they use paddles from nine to ten feet long, and they can travel in their primitive craft from thirty to forty miles a day. At first experience of a dug-out one feels very unsafe. If one has to cough, for example, one is apt to do so along the lines of the boat, for it seems that to cough sideways would be of a certainty to capsize it.

The Old Drift of this time was a very small settlement of about a dozen white men round two or three stores right on the river bank. In the rainy season it was a swamp. I shall have more to say of it later, when in my narrative I get back from my trip into the interior. I would say here, however, that in all the vast territory of North-western Rhodesia in 1903 there were no more than, if as much as, a hundred white people. It wasn't until the following year that the railway reached Victoria Falls, and the want of it, of course, kept down the number of people entering Northern Rhodesia. At the beginning of the century North-western Rhodesia and North-eastern Rhodesia were separate territories, each having its own Administration. Now they are amalgamated and administered as one. To show the expansion after the coming of the railway, perhaps I may quote some figures. In 1911, according to the census, the population of the two northern Rhodesias in whites (European) was 1497. The area of the territory over which this population was distributed was 287,950 square miles, which means that there was about one white man to every 200 square miles. Twenty years later, in 1931, the white population was 13,846—about one white person to every 20 square miles. But to return to my story:

After crossing the drift, one of the local stores, which was also an hotel, had to be visited. Our stocks had to be replenished and carriers engaged for our trip up-river. The owner of this store was the original white settler. He was of the same name as myself, except that his had the aristocratic ' e ' hitched to it. This might have been point of contact enough for us, but we hadn't been chatting together many minutes before I found that he came from Chatteris in Cambridgeshire. It seemed that I couldn't get away from the old county.

Our immediate objective from the Old Drift was Kasangula, whence we meant to set out in dug-outs for

BAOBAB-TREE NEAR THE FALLS

124

Lia-Lui, four hundred miles up the Zambesi. Kasangula was a sixty-mile trek. We could not reach it by boat, because the river for fifty miles above the Old Drift was one quick succession of rapids. Among our carriers for this part of the journey were three men of the Mashu-kulumbwe, a tribe that wore no clothes. These men travelled stark naked and, though it was bitterly cold at nights, had no blankets. When we asked why they wore no clothes they merely said, " We are not women." The trek to Kasangula was by easy-going, level ground, with the track never far from the river, so that there was no shortage of water. We completed the trek in two and a half days, passing but one kraal, Maponda's, about fifteen miles from Kasangula.

At Kasangula there was a fairly large kraal bossed by an old chief called Quinani. This was a quaint old bird who spent his time squatting on the ground outside his enclosure, basking in the sun and snuffing at frequent and regular intervals. As long as the sun shone, there he sat, day in and day out, dressed in a leopard skin and a red and white woollen skull-cap.

We camped under the big trees of Kasangula and tried to hire dug-outs from this old chieftain for our trip up-river. For the main voyaging no boats were available. All Quinani's boats were away on some expedition and would not be back for some days. But O'Connor, who was anxious to push on ahead and get a store built at Lia-Lui before his goods arrived—they were in transit from Bulawayo to the Zambesi—managed to secure a single dug-out and got off right away.

The enforced inaction troubled me little. I was quite snug in my camp under the trees with no chance of rain until the next October or November, and I contented myself with some fishing and shooting.

The fishing was excellent. There were tiger fish, which give much the same play as pike in home waters and are as sweet eating. They have, however, too many fine bones to be popular as a dish. The two largest of these fish that I have seen caught weighed 17½ and 14 pounds. They take spoons and live-bait quite readily, and their favourite haunts are in the rapids or near them.

It was a surprise to me to find bream taking readily to the spoon. But the Zambesi bream is an accommodating fellow, for he takes live-bait or small fish cut up, loves worms, and snatches at bread paste. He makes excellent eating and is as delicate as a sole when properly cooked. His fillets, skinned and bread-crumbed, are delicious when fried in butter.

The shooting, too, was very good—and very varied. There were guinea-fowl, pheasant and partridge, and koran to be had to landward, while on the river there were geese and ducks of various sorts. Wild turkeys also were to be got. The country teemed with food that was to be had for the shooting, and abounded in game from the stately eland and sable antelope down to the tiny oribi.

One evening I went out to get a bird for dinner. It was close to sunset. In a thicket of long grass I heard guinea-fowl calling and, going quite close, I loosed off a barrel in the direction of the sound. A flight of about a dozen got up, and I saw a couple were wounded, but I couldn't get off my second barrel because of the trees. I went, however, to see if my random shot had got me a

126

dinner. To my amazement I found I had accounted for six guinea-fowl, surely a record for one cartridge.

One way or another my sojourn at Kasangula was full of incident. I once saw a naked savage tied to a stake driven into the ground. On asking what he was tied up for I was told that he was a murderer awaiting execution. When and where he was executed I cannot say, but next time I saw the stake it was vacant.

I might say, in passing, that at this time I knew nothing of the Barotse language, but got along with some of the natives who could talk what was called Kitchen Kaffir. With this I was fairly conversant. Some time later I came across a Barotse who had learnt English. He gave me a long list of words with their meanings, together with some idea of the grammar, and from this start I was able after a time to get along fairly well in Barotse.

I was having tea one afternoon, about two days after my arrival at Kasangula, when a coloured man came along and told me that a white man was dying at Maponda's kraal. I said I would be along as soon as I finished my tea. As I was finishing, however, there appeared on the scene a long, lanky Scotsman. He was draped with arms and ammunition, and he was followed by a native who carried a large basket. The Scot came right up to me and, without any preliminary greeting or palaver, made an announcement.

" You've a hellofa lot of lions round here."

" I haven't seen any," said I.

" Well—I've just seen a hundred or so over there."

I received this surprising statement with fairish calm.

"Have a cup of tea," I suggested, "and we'll get busy."

"No tea, thanks. Gimme a drink!"

"Don't carry it," I told him. I had, in fact, only one bottle of brandy for medicinal purposes on my six months' trip. By this time I could see that my visitor was in that condition sometimes called 'the rats.' His next demand was barked out.

"Gimme five quid!"

"Nothing doing," I replied. "I don't carry money with me on these trips."

"Can you shoot?" he barked. And began fumbling in the basket which the bearer had put near him on the ground.

"A bit," I admitted. Leaning over my pillow I put myself into the way of grabbing my ·450.

"Well—you'll have to in a minute," said he. And then I did grab my ·450, covering him from my reclining position, for he seemed to be working up to madness.

Luckily, however, he eased off a bit after that. I gave him some Bovril and got him to lie down. I talked to him soothingly and managed to coax him into a rest hut near by. After some time he fell into a troubled sleep, and his boy and myself took the chance of removing his rifle and shot-gun and hiding them in the bush. Then we searched his basket and found a hunting-knife. This, too, we hid.

The visitor's troubled sleep did not last long. Almost no sooner had we got his weapons cached than he was up, raving mad. He found a cut-throat razor which we had missed in his basket, and flourishing this he started to chase my boys about, threatening to murder them. I

THE CHASM FROM THE WESTERN END OF THE FALLS

managed to get him back to the hut, but he would not let me out of his sight. If I moved he became excited again, so I had to stay by him. It wasn't until the evening, when he fell into a decent sort of sleep, that I could attempt to get away. I was, it may be imagined, fed up with the task of playing ' Fido ' to a drunken, delirious stranger; once I got outside the hut I barricaded him into it with as many and as weighty things as I could find, and went off to my own bed.

There was a sudden uproar in the middle of the night. Bellowings and yells went up in the rest hut. One terrific charge, and door, barricade, and everything went flying. My patient, so to call him, barged out and headed straight for the river. Into the water he leapt. I ran after him, but stopped short on the bank. Fortunately there were no crocodiles about, for he was up to his neck in water for some time before my persuasion had effect in getting him out of it.

I had five days of this before I got him back to normal. By then I was exhausted by wear and tear. I had a heart-to-heart talk then with the sober Mac. I learned that he had been on a glorious bend at the Old Drift and that he hadn't a bean left. I made it clear to him that it was no use going to Barotse without cash, and persuaded him to return whence he had come. He went south as persuaded, and I gave him a fiver.

Six months later I was sitting chatting with one or two men in the hotel yard at the Old Drift when a fellow breezed up.

" You're Percy Clark, aren't you? " he said to me.

I owned up, but said it wasn't my fault. I was born that way.

"I owe you some money," he said.

"You're a liar," said I. "I've never set eyes on you before."

"Oh, yes, you have," he returned. "Mean to say you don't remember Kasangula six months back?"

"Why, yes! You're the fellow that had 'em. You're Mac!"

"That's me," he said, and stuck out his hand to shake. "And here's your fiver," said he.

CHAPTER X

UP THE ZAMBESI

THE dug-outs of Quinani returned at long last. I hired five of them to take me and my goods up-river as far as Sesheke. This was a large kraal occupied by Litia, the heir to the paramount chief, Lewanika. The trip, which I took in leisurely fashion, lasted three days. Many hippos were encountered and crocodiles were seen by the score.

Some fifteen miles from Sesheke itself we came to the Simorrocco Flats, a piece of country as flat as the back of one's hand. At that time of the year it was covered with long dry grass. Thousands of mixed game could be seen and separate herds numbering hundreds. It was here that I shot my first buck. He was a large lechwe, with beautiful curved horns of black with a golden sheen.

I went ashore with my rifle. About eight hundred yards off I saw a couple of lechwe, a buck and a doe. The buck was facing my way with his head raised. He appeared to be looking straight at me. The doe stood sideways, broadside on, as it were. There was no stalking game on those flats, so I walked straight towards the couple, the grass—very coarse and as big as reeds—making what seemed an infernal row. When I had got nearer by about three hundred yards the doe fled, leaving the buck still facing in my direction.

It was a Martini I had—a rifle that fired a very heavy

bullet; it was very greatly favoured by the Dutchmen in those days. I thought I would try a shot from where I was, so dropping to one knee and sighting for 500 yards, I took careful aim. I fired, but missed. Strange to say, the buck did not move, but still stood gazing in my direction. I reckoned that my missing was due to a slight wind, so I used the wind-gauge for correction. This time I did not miss. The buck fell. I walked up to it and found I had drilled it clean between the eyes— though I say it myself, a magnificent shot. The buck was a very useful addition to the larder, for I had the boys to feed.

At Sesheke there were two stores, one run by a Jew and the other by an Englishman. There was also a newly appointed District Commissioner, fresh out from Oxford. I made camp on the veldt to stop at Sesheke for two weeks, and I made friends with those three whites, as also with a couple of prospectors who were going on a long expedition into the interior for the Northern Copper Company.

The terrier bitch that I had acquired at Wankie—I called her Flossie—by this time had become my inseparable companion. I could not have had a better pal. One night, when I was sleeping as usual on the veldt, a terrific uproar arose a few yards from my bed. Pots and pans were rattling, and it was apparent that Flossie was having a great fight among the culinary ware. The sounds were heavy enough to suggest a lion, so I grabbed my rifle and hopped out of my blankets. Two animals' forms could dimly be discerned milling round, one much bigger than the other. I could not risk putting in a shot, lest I should slay my best friend—but as I made for the battle area the bigger animal loped off. Then I could see it was a jackal that had evidently been prowling round for stray bits of food.

Hyenas and jackals made the nights hideous with their howling. It was melancholy and unremitting. One ached to hear them take three bars rest, but they never did. Fortunately, there are conditions where one gets used to anything.

The two prospectors I have mentioned, Dick Carlisle and Billy Butcher, were both pioneers of Southern Rhodesia. Colonial born, they were the best of good fellows, splendid shots, jolly-natured—and good friends to me, a raw hand in an uncivilized country. We arranged between us for a shooting trip of three days on the Simorrocco Flats.

One morning early we started off. We went up a tributary of the Zambesi, the Kesia river, for a couple of miles and made camp at a place where the river bent. It was a good spot and we had a splendid bag. Usually we were up before sunrise and, after a cup of coffee and a biscuit, we would start off in different directions to get among the game before the sun came up. By ten o'clock we would be back in camp for breakfast, and the rest of the day—until time for the evening shoot, after which we had our only other meal—would be passed in skinning our kill, fishing, or shooting crocodiles. The Kesia river simply teemed with these brutes. I had never imagined there could be so many in one place. It appeared to me that they patrolled the river in twos or threes. There were hundreds of them. Once, sitting on the river bank, I counted over twenty of them with their heads above water. I could not make out how they fed.

We threw a jackal into the river one day, thinking it would be snapped up, but next morning it was still floating about, untouched.

On the second morning, in the pearly grey of the dawn, it was slightly misty. Looking across the river I saw on the far side a big herd of antelope moving at what looked like a mile away at a gentle trot. I pointed them out to Dick and Billy, and the three of us set out across the river in a dug-out with our rifles. We approached cautiously, but we had not gone a hundred yards when we saw that our herd of antelopes was nothing other than a flock of guinea-fowl. The dim light and the morning mist had created an illusion to deceive even such old stagers as my prospector friends.

By the second evening we had a quantity of nice hides pegged out to dry. They were to be cut into *reimpjes*—hide strips that were a substitute for ropes and useful for many purposes. That night we were aroused by the boat-boys yelling that the veldt was on fire. Awake, we became aware of danger. The blaze was all about us and coming towards us. We could have escaped to the dug-outs, but that meant leaving tents, goods, blankets, and most of our possessions, for there was no time to remove them. Our position was made the more perilous by the fact that we were in a bend of the river. With no time to spare, we all grabbed the thing nearest to us that might serve for beating out the flames. Some got tree-branches, others pulled up the pegged-out hides. These last were excellent for beating out the fire. For two solid hours we fought without a breathing spell, and in the end we won. Our camp was saved. But what a sight we were! Black and grimy, utterly fagged out.

MY PROSPECTOR FRIENDS

Dick is standing; Billy is on the right.

Our skins—the animal hides, I mean—were ruined. But we were full of satisfaction. We had saved our camp.

The next afternoon we packed up and set out for home—by which I mean Sesheke—leaving the corpses of many crocs lying about behind us. The atmosphere of that bend of the Kesia must have been extremely juicy three days later.

Soon after we reached the Zambesi on our way home we came across a school of hippos. I was very keen to have a shot at one, and suggested stopping. The old hands, however, said it would be useless. The hippos were too far out in the river. If shot at, they would only come up at intervals to breathe, though in general they showed their heads above water for long periods.

I had a few rounds of ammunition left, and I said I meant to have a shot at them anyhow. I was put ashore, and Billy and Dick went on with a " See you later ! " It seemed to me that the hippos were about three hundred yards out, and I sighted my rifle for that distance. One of the beasts was gazing landward. I took careful aim at him, fired—and missed. After this it was snap-shooting at momentarily appearing heads. I marked the spot where one particular head appeared and drew a bead on it. The head came up and I fired. Another miss. Still I waited for the reappearance of the same head, and fired a third time. The natives with me declared I had hit the hippo, but I was not at all sure. With another two shots at other heads my ammunition was exhausted. I left a boy to watch if the supposed hit had really taken effect. It takes some four hours for a dead hippo to be brought to the surface by distension from internal gases.

I got back to Sesheke for dinner at the store, and I told my companions my story. " Did it make an awful commotion and splash about? " I was asked. " No," I replied, " it merely disappeared." " Then," was the verdict, " you didn't hit it."

This all goes to show that even old hands " never can tell." Before we got to bed the native I had left behind turned up with the news that the hippo was dead and floating. We decided to get up early in the morning and go to retrieve it. Sure enough, next morning we found the beast bobbing around much in the same spot as where he had been shot. It was no easy task pushing him with paddles on to a sandbank, for a hippo weighs close on two tons. However, by dint of great exertion we got him ashore at long last. The next thing to do was skin him and cut him up. He was by this time well blown up and had to be deflated. An assegai did the trick—and, oh!—the scent was horrible. The air seemed to turn blue and thick enough for cutting. But the natives, at least, appeared to revel in it—as though they would have eaten their mealies with the smell and have enjoyed it.

The Barotse love hippo meat, however, and they will travel almost any distance on a chance of getting some.

I had a letter from O'Connor, three hundred miles up-river, a fortnight later. It was written the day after I shot the hippo and was brought down by a runner. But O'Connor wrote that he had heard I had shot a hippo. Here was an instance of the rapidity with which news travels among the natives. O'Connor could write of hearing of my hippo a few hours after it came to the surface of the river, while it took the runner two weeks to bring me his letter. I still ask myself how it is done, this sort of thing. That night I heard nothing out of the way in the beating of tom-toms. It is well known, of course, that during the Boer war natives knew the result of engagements long before the whites could hear.

There was another instance of hippo news within my own experience. I shot one at a place about twenty miles from the nearest kraal. Within three hours natives from this kraal were hurrying down to the river anxious for a share of the meat. At this time I had sixty boys to feed, and the hippo meat came in very useful other than directly, for the natives who wanted a share of the meat brought as barter such edibles as fowls, sweet potatoes, mealies, pumpkins, and so forth—all of which gave my boys a needed change of diet. That is perhaps beside the point I wanted to make. So far none has discovered the native method of spreading news at this quite amazing speed.

The kraal of Litia at Sesheke contained about two thousand natives. Close by it was another large kraal. This was ruled over by the ' Little Mokwae '—or Little Queen of the Barotse. The Little Queen's mother, the ' Big Mokwae,' lived at Nalalo, nearly three hundred miles up the river. The Big Queen, an enormous woman physically, is believed to have been born in 1832. She died in 1934.

The Big Queen, Mokwae Matuka, ruled jointly with Lewanika, the Barotse king. They were brother and sister, so that the Little Queen, Mokwae Akanakisa, was the future queen. She was a very hard case indeed, as I hope to show.

While I was in Sesheke I was asked by the Little Queen to take her photograph. This I was ready enough to do, because later on I wanted to hire dug-outs from her. I sent word that I would be at the Palace—so-called —at a certain time on a certain day. When the time came, to make sure I hadn't forgotten, she sent her Prime Minister, her Secretary (who claimed to speak English), and a guard of honour to escort me to the Palace.

This ' statelified ' arrival of mine was on time, but, as is common with her sex, her Majesty was late. I sent for her twice, but the first time the excuse was " she go wash, also a dress," and then " she come now." A further quarter of an hour went by, and by then my patience gave out completely. I left the camp in high dudgeon.

Almost before I got out a messenger came after me to say that the queen was now ready. I told him to convey to her Majesty the information that I was a white man and that I would not be treated like a Kaffir. Then I went home.

Shortly after that a runner arrived with a letter addressed to " Mr Clark, Esq." It was very humble and apologetic. So much so that eventually I agreed to turn up again next day, which I did. After a lecture on the comparative dignity of black and white, I took the portrait.

The next day I received from the queen a present of an ox and a carved bowl filled with thick milk. I appreciated the bowl rather more than the rest of the present, but later on a messenger arrived with greeting from the

BEATING TOM-TOMS OUTSIDE LITIA'S PALACE

138

queen—and would I kindly return the bowl when I had finished the milk? At the same time I received an invitation to dinner, which I accepted.

This dinner was the first I had ever eaten with a native, and it went rather against the grain to accept. But, as I say, I wanted boats later on, so I went.

I was thankful I had taken Flossie with me. I dined alone with the Queen, and the meal was a simple one, much to my satisfaction. I don't know what training the Queen's *chef* had experienced, for his meat was about 'the limit' for toughness. One mouthful was enough for me, and to keep up appearances and to get rid of the meat at the same time was a doubly tough proposition. This was where Flossie became useful. The toughness of the meat bothered her none, and she had a real good feed.

But I wanted to tell you what a hard case Mokwae was. Here is one instance. When in the presence of royalty the natives had to go down on their knees and clap their hands in salutation. Her Majesty had been given a supply of tea, together with a tea service, by one of the traders, and she was very proud of the outfit. The first time the tea was brewed it was brought in by one of the servants. When the girl was approaching the Queen, she got into a fix over presenting the tea-tray and clapping her hands at the same time. She tried to do both together, with the result that the tray was dropped and the crockery smashed. The Queen was so riled that she took up an assegai and stabbed the culprit. This happened before I arrived at Sesheke.

An episode that was recounted to me after my return from up-country is perhaps more amusing. Mokwae

Akanakisa at different times had taken unto herself two husbands, both chosen for her by King Lewanika. She found connubial bliss lasted not very long with either, and she discarded them.

Lewanika sent down a third husband with a stern message that he was to be the last and that she must stick to him. The third fellow did not please her Majesty at all, and she declined him with thanks. But she was so mad about it all that she started ructions on a large scale. She got all her indunas, or chiefs, together with their wives, and began an enforced swopping match. As a result an old induna with three or four antique wives would find himself in possession of strapping wenches in substitution, while a young chief would be faced with the prospect of having old hags. Naturally the indunas objected to the arrangement, and refused to make the swop. Whereupon the Queen declared a state of mutiny and had the objectors tied up for throwing to the crocodiles. Fortunately, however, Litia appeared at this crucial juncture and contrived to smooth matters.

During my stay at Sesheke I made friends with Litia. He was a well-educated man, having been taught by the missionaries, and he was very keen on photography. The traders were always giving presents to keep in good favour for business purposes, and one of them had given Litia a camera. I helped him a good deal with his photography. He had fixed up a dark-room, with water for the developing and for the washing of prints kept in enormous brown clay jars. These kept the water wonderfully cool.

When I was leaving Sesheke, Litia presented me with

a beautiful leopard skin and asked me to stay on and teach him more. I said that nothing would suit me better, but that I couldn't afford it. " How much would you want to stop? " he asked. I said that thirty pounds a month would tempt me, and that I would take it in cattle. This, by the way, was not so cheap as it may seem. There the price of beasts ranged from sixteen shillings to twenty-eight shillings a head, but herded to Francistown, though that was a good distance off, they would fetch from seven pounds to ten pounds apiece. Litia thought for a long time, then replied sadly, " *Hahooloohooloo!* " Which is to say, " Too much! "

I have remarked on the number of crocodiles in the river. They infested it by Sesheke, and women and children fetching water were commonly taken by them. Nothing was done about it until one day a chief was snatched, and then a defence against the brutes was set up. Poles were cut, and an enclosure made with them, taking in a good part of the river and with sides carried well up the bank, the entrance being at the highest point. This reduced the number of deaths considerably.

Once when strolling by the river I surprised a group of natives. They were under a high bank performing a weird ceremonial. I watched them for a time unseen, then showed myself. I asked them the meaning of the incantations and the ritual. It was only after a deal of persuasion that I got my own boy to tell me. The natives were about to take some cattle, by swimming, to an island in midstream and they were doing *moreane*, or ' medicine,' to the river-god to stop the crocs from taking the cattle in crossing.

Before I left Sesheke I had a business offer from the

Jew trader who ran one of the two stores there. He was at need to leave Barotseland on account of bad health, and he thought it would be a good idea for me to take over the store and its contents. I was to pay him when I had disposed of the stock, or sooner if I liked. The idea had its attractions, and I took over some days before he was due to depart. But I hadn't been in possession more than a day or two when another Jew came along, and I was told that this second fellow was to help me in running the store. No such assistance was needed, and I became indignant. I told the owner that I was not going to be watched, and that he could go and eat coke. Then I walked out. The storekeeper departed a day or two after that, and the second Jew was left in charge. Perhaps I needn't say that every bob he took while running things was a prisoner. Much later this same store was taken over by two brothers of the same persuasion. To-day these two men are about the richest in Northern Rhodesia.

I reverted to my original plan of going farther up-country, and on the eve of my departure a farewell banquet was given by my friend the English trader. Litia was invited, with my two prospector pals. During the evening Litia was asked to sing something in his own language. Standing up solemnly he sang something to the old tune of *Abide with Me*. Up to now I haven't decided whether Litia was being a humorist or merely sentimental.

I had secured some dug-outs for the journey. Dick and Billy were leaving at the same time. Much to my satisfaction they agreed to let me travel with them. I was making for Lia-Lui, where the King's kraal of ten

LITIA

thousand natives was located. Litia asked me to call on his father, Lewanika, and to convey his greetings to him. This I readily promised to do.

I may jump ahead a few weeks here to the capital and tell what happened when I went to convey Litia's greetings. On the morning that I called the King was holding court—that is, listening to his subjects who had come to make complaints and to have their quarrels adjusted, seeking the King's justice. The court was cleared of litigants and wrongdoers on my arrival. The King, with his Prime Minister and council and interpreter in attendance, received me at once.

After salutations and greetings had been exchanged, and the royal beer made of honey had been consumed, conversation went freely for a time. Then the King turned to the interpreter.

" What does Mr Clark want? " he asked.

" Nothing," I replied. " I am here on a simple visit to your capital, and came to bring you greeting from your son."

The King seemed puzzled. A few minutes later his query was repeated, and I gave the same reply.

" Well," said Lewanika, not without wonder, " this is the first white man to visit me that has not asked me for something! "

If he had spoken volumes, surely, he could not have made more eloquent comment on white concession-hunters.

CHAPTER XI

UP-RIVER AND DOWN AGAIN

THE journey up the Zambesi to Lia-Lui was not very eventful. I did shoot my second hippo, but in a routine way. There was, however, other shooting.

One afternoon, after making camp in the usual way at about four o'clock, we went out with our rifles. I was on my own when I heard a shot in the distance. Directly after that a herd of impala came thundering towards me. It was a wonderful sight. There must have been nearly three thousand in the herd, jumping high as they came—and they are marvellous jumpers. I got behind a tree and waited until they got within good range, then I selected a fine buck and fired. As far as I could make out I had missed. The beasts halted at the sound of my shot. I picked out another buck and dropped him. Off thundered the herd, and I went over to my kill. To my surprise I found that my first shot had found its mark, and that I had bagged two buck.

Two hundred and fifty miles above the Victoria Falls we came to those of N'gonye. They are very beautiful. They consist of a series of cataracts and one large horse-shoe fall, where the water plunges over a drop of about seventy feet and into a short run of gorge below. I don't know whether the Rev. Mr Coillard, the first missionary in Barotseland, photographed this lovely sight. If not, I was the first man to take a picture of the N'gonye Falls.

Lovely though the Falls were, they meant a portage. A day was spent in hauling the dug-outs up round to above the Falls and carrying our goods. The lone trader here was a Dutchman, and he spent the evening with us. A lively customer in any case, he could not bear to go to bed while there was anyone to talk to. I retired early. I was sleeping on the ground, and had placed my clothes alongside my bed. In my coat pocket was one of my most treasured possessions carefully brought all the way from Bulawayo. This was an Irish clay pipe which I had coloured beautifully. Of course the Dutchman, mucking about, had to jump on my coat and smash my lovely pipe. In the course of my life I've had losses of infinitely greater intrinsic value, but there is none I remember being more annoyed about than that. It quite spoiled my immediate satisfaction with the N'gonye Falls.

Farther up the river we saw another magnificent sight. This was the nesting-place for some thousands of birds of a particular species. It was in an overhanging part of the bank, the only place on the river where, at that time, this specimen was to be seen. Our passing put them up in their hundreds, and with their vivid plumage they looked like the myriad shuttles of some rainbow-weaving loom, a wonderful and dazzling thing to see.

Before we got to Lia-Lui we came to a place where one of the kings was buried. Our boys could not pass the spot without landing to make an offering to the spirit of the dead, and to give the royal salute. They maintained that if they passed without this ceremony some harm would befall them. But royalty, dead or alive, is regarded with great reverence in Barotseland. Royal folks, it is believed, are born of Nyambe, the Barotse divinity. The king and queen are held to be demi-gods, and the belief persists in most parts of Barotseland to this day. The monarchs are not only above the common people; they are above the law.

We arrived ultimately at Lia-Lui. My friends Dick and Billy went off west on their hazardous prospecting trip, which they did not bring to a finish until twelve months later. They were the best of good fellows, those two, and I wish even now that I had accompanied them into the unknown. But, one way and another, I missed the opportunity.

The British Government was represented at Lia-Lui by one District Commissioner, a Mr Aitkin, with whom I stayed at Mongu, not far from the King's kraal. He was, I believe, the first one to start a real garden in this part of the world, growing fruit, flowers, and vegetables. When I was with him he was much taken up with cultivating pineapples.

The King's kraal was full of interest. It was situated in a valley which was always flooded in the rainy season. At this time of year the whole population of some ten thousand migrate to a sand belt a mile or two away. The King must be the first to leave, and none is allowed to precede him. Before the King gets on the move his subjects in the kraal are in a bad way, for the royal progress is made, traditionally, in a royal barge—and that needs quite a depth of water before it can float.

The barge is an enormous affair about sixty feet in length. In its middle are two compartments, a living-room and a sleeping-room, both roofed over. An elephant decorates the roof, and this elephant is chief 'prop' for a lot of mummery on the part of the court

DUG-OUTS ON THE WAY TO LIA-LUI

jester, who pretends to hunt and shoot it, cutting extra-ordinary capers the while, to the intense amusement of the populace. Besides this functionary, with others of the retinue, accommodation is made on the barge for a band of some twenty musicians with their weird and wonderful instruments—one might say—of torture. Then from fifty to sixty paddlers are required to propel the barge, and a host of bailers to keep it seaworthy. It may be grasped that the journey to the sand-bank, made to the accompaniment of strange music and barbaric song, is a slow business. The return is made four or five months later.

It was interesting to note the native ways of dealing with their grain supply. All kraals had their granaries of one sort or another. In the King's kraal the granaries occupied a large area, and they consisted of miniature huts perched ten feet above the ground on poles. Here the mealie cobs were kept. When meal was wanted cobs to the required amount were taken out and stripped of their grains. These were put into a stamping-mill which was made out of a section of tree about four foot high, hollowed out to about half-way down and with a solid base. The stamping was done as a rule by two women. The whole grains, or mealies, having been poured into the hollow bowl of the mill, the women got to work with a thick, heavy pole apiece, which they brought down, end on and alternately, with all their force, crushing the grain.

In the next process the crushed grain is taken from the stamping-mill and put on a large stone. Other women, for work is always done by the females, begin further to pulverize the grain, rolling it with a large upper stone

147

until it is a fine powder. In the course of time the nether stone is hollowed out with this continual grinding. It will be seen that this way of grinding mealies, Kaffir corn, and so on, is merely a primitive version of our own old windmill process.

The Matabele method of storing grain differs from the Barotse. The people on the other and lower side of the Zambesi make clay receptacles, about five to six feet high, not unlike a postal pillar-box. These have no openings except at the top, and the openings are just large enough for the insertion of the contents. When one of these little granaries is filled, another is constructed. One can—or one could in the early days—see them peppered all about the Matabele kraals.

By the time I got to Lia-Lui my friend O'Connor was ready to open his store. Permission to trade had to be asked of the King, and his Majesty was the first customer. Most of the trading was by barter, cows and oxen being brought to pay for the trade goods, but the King demanded cash-money for his beasts when he came to declare the store open. His Majesty announced the time of his arrival beforehand, and sent ahead of him three large oxen, which he priced at ten pounds per head. O'Connor could not kick about these arrangements and demands. If he had, it would have been good-bye to all hope of trading with Lewanika's subjects. When his Majesty arrived he received his money and began to buy.

But even with the King's exorbitant demands, my friend was not so badly off in the long run. The profits on trade goods were enormous in those days. Cups and saucers — the sort one got with " A present from

Margate " on them—fetched ten shillings each. Spoons
went at the same ratio, three-halfpenny spoons for a
shilling apiece. Japanese silk fetched ten shillings a yard.
Yes, trading was a great game in Barotseland in 1903,
but the money made at it was generally soon spent.

At that time the witch-doctor was still ' doing his
stuff. ' He was a weird spectacle, decorated in ways
beyond detailing, with tails of animals, charms round
his neck, bones and bangles on his arms and ankles, and
with parts of his body showing in between. Dancing and
shouting to the sound of tom-toms and other so-called
musical instruments, he was a fearsome sight—or
thought he was. To-day the witch-doctors are suppressed by law, but the practice of throwing the bones
and smelling-out still exists.

The Barotse were a powerful nation with conquered
tribes paying tribute to them. If the subjected failed to
bring in their tribute, penalties were exacted from them
in unpleasant fashion. I have seen such natives whose
ears were almost cut off, all but completely severed and
hanging by the cartilage close to the lobe. This, with the
slitting and cutting off of noses, was by no means the
most drastic of punishments for the non-payment of
tribute. There were other inflictions that cannot be
written. But the day of these things, one may thank
God, has gone for good.

I had no white companion on my return journey down
the Zambesi. But for the native boys I wandered alone
about the country, exploring the river's tributaries, in a
go-as-you-please sort of style. I had a small fleet of
dug-outs.

A few days after I left Lewaniki's kraal a runner came for me carrying a batch of letters which had been sent on by the solitary official Postmaster in North-western Rhodesia. The fact that the runner came for me alone may indicate how few whites there were in the territory: I took it as a great compliment. The native had travelled over four hundred miles to find me, and it may be imagined how welcome the letters were to me.

My main problem was the food supply for my sixty native boys. All I could give them was the meat I shot. I have mentioned hippo meat. It always was a good addition to the larder, but for vegetables we had to forage. We could always get a good supply, with pumpkins, milk, sweet potatoes, and so forth, in exchange for the meat. So we were really self-supporting. After shooting a hippo I would camp on the spot for the purpose of making biltong, a sort of ' buccanning ' process. The meat of the hippo was cut into strips and dried in the sun for future use. The hide also was treated. It too was cut into strips and stretched on green saplings for making into sjamboks.

Besides the meat of a hippo, one gets two or three buckets of fat from it by rendering. This, after one gets used to the flavour, is very good for cooking. The meat itself I could never care for, though it is not unlike ordinary beef. I tried the tongue, the feet, and various joints from time to time, but hippo takes a deuce of a lot of cooking, it seems. The tongue, for example, I boiled for hours, but it still was tough. I tried roasting joints, boiling joints, and stewing joints, and never rescued the meat from appalling toughness. The natives,

PORTAGE AT N'GONYE FALLS

Flossie in the foreground.

however, appear to value it more than any kind of meat food. Buck meat and the flesh of birds are good enough for me on the veldt.

On the matter of change of diet, one day I saw the boys cooking eggs. They were the size of goose eggs, and looked as appetizing as eggs may be. The boys told me they were crocodile eggs, and that their flavour was simply delicious. They presented me with a few, which were cooked for my breakfast next morning. One mouthful was enough. Take equal portions of rotten domestic eggs, rotten fish, rotten cabbage; stir in carbon-disulphide for seasoning. You will then have some notion of what croc eggs taste like. It is thirty years since I tasted that egg, and I can still recall the flavour.

In all this time weeks would pass before I encountered a white man. I had to keep the white prestige alive, and at times it was rather difficult.

One afternoon we arrived at some rapids that were about a mile in extent. In the first days of my down-stream trip, when rapids were encountered I would leave the boats and walk until clear water was reached. The boys were fearful of drowning me if the boat upset. But after two extended walks down-river I made up my mind that padding it wasn't good enough, and that I might as well have as much fun as was going. And I stuck to the boat, not to any apparent delight on the part of the boys.

On this afternoon, before attempting to shoot the rapids, I let the boys have a rest on an island. Wanting to negotiate the rapids before dark, I suggested we should get a move on. " Nothing doing! " the boys said, in effect. " We'll see about that," I said, showing my

·450 Webley. " Get a move on ! " I selected my personal crew and drove them one by one at revolver point into the boat. Then I turned to the remainder, about forty of them.

" I am going now," I said. " You can stop here until morning, if you like, but if you do there will be no more skoff for you from me on the journey. You will have to find food for yourselves. That's all ! "

I made camp at the foot of the rapids. Towards sun- down first one boat arrived, then another, and another, till at last the whole fleet was with me. When the last boy had turned up, I got the whole gang of them into line and gave them a lecture. Then I made them all kneel and rub their foreheads in the dust and give the royal salute That finished the ' indaba.' I had got them on their weakest spot, their bellies.

The banks of the Zambesi are lined for miles here and there with papyrus and reeds, often to a depth of fifty yards, making it impossible to land. One night, after travelling for miles in search of an opening by which I could get to firm earth, I found myself stranded along- side those weeds. I decided to camp in a hippo run, which is no more than a tunnel through the reeds. This, I may say, was decidedly dangerous, for a hippo might come through the tunnel on his way to the river or to land. There was, however, no alternative for me. I built a small fire in the run, a proceeding which increased the danger rather than diminished it. The hippo has a way of making for a fire to trample it out. All night we could hear the hippos splashing and bellowing up and down the river, but fortunately none took it into his big head to use that particular tunnel. I was in a blue funk all night and slept mighty little. As far as the splashing and bellowing of the hippos went, there was nothing unusual. They had such bathing parties every night.

The Barotse are very fond of fish, dried or fresh. Apart from netting, their main method was spearing. They would take a dug-out and pull along the reeds, there being one of them with an assegai in the bows. If this fellow saw a fish he stabbed at it in the water, and nine times out of ten not only hit the mark but secured the fish. In ordinary travelling, besides the two to four paddlers at the stern, there was always a man in the bows to steer. They all stood to their work. The fellow in the bows carried an assegai as well as his paddle, and if he saw a fish would spear it in passing.

At times fish eagles could be seen. They were enormous birds, beautiful in the pure white of their breasts. Hovering high over the water, they would suddenly drop into it like a stone, reappearing with a fish weighing anything from one to five pounds. They would then take their prey to a rock and devour it. On occasions the boys would see one of these birds at such a meal. Then they would paddle towards it, shouting. The eagle would fly off, and the boys would secure what was left of the fish.

The crocodiles, as already said, were numerous. In the dug-out it was possible to steal past them quietly as they lay sunning on the sandbanks, and it was interesting to see how they kept their powerful jaws wide open, what time a bird hopped about in the gape picking food from between the teeth. This bird, they say, is never injured, the crocs recognizing its usefulness as a toothpick.

One of the oddest sights I saw was out on the veldt at a native kraal that I came on while shooting. Surrounded by a crowd, a native was reclining on the ground with another sitting by him. Alongside was a wooden bowl containing, I should say, over a pint of blood. The patient was extremely emaciated, and his body from neck to feet was covered with cuts. The cupping was still going on when I turned up, there being about half a dozen rams' horns still attached to the patient's body. When half full of blood the horns dropped off, and the contents were emptied into the bowl. Then another cut was made and the cupping continued. I did not wait for the inquest.

One of the superstitions among the boys of the Upper Zambesi is that whistling calls up a wind. My own boat boys did not like my frequent habit of whistling when cheerful, though I did it merely because I had nobody to talk to. They declared that the wind would surely come and upset the dug-out. One day, indeed, when I was cheerfully whistling, a sudden squall did upset one of the boats in midstream. The boat sank with its cargo of five bags of grain, but no lives were lost. Although I was nowhere near the boat at the time, I was accused of causing it to be lost. I had, incidentally, to pay for it. From world travellers I have learned that the same superstition is held in all directions to the remotest corners of the globe, and one knows, of course, that British seamen believe in it. It would be interesting to discover whence such a general superstition arose.

Far from the nearest white man, and two hundred miles from the nearest settlement, I ran across a native blacksmith. The forge was in the open under a large

THE NELA KWANDA

State barge of Lewanika, Paramount Chief of the Barotse.

Photo by A. S. O'Connor

shady tree, and the blacksmith was very old. He had an assistant almost as aged. The furnace was a hollow in the ground filled with charcoal of their own manufacture. The bellows was made of two wooden bowls set side by side, each covered by a parchment. Through each parchment came a stick, and this was used to raise and lower each parchment alternately. Attached to the underside of each bowl was a clay pipe that conveyed the blast to the furnace. The heat raised by this primitive apparatus was remarkable. The anvil was a conical piece of iron stuck well into the ground with a round top about three inches in diameter. It was the assistant's duty to work the bellows, which he did with the bowls between his legs. The boss also worked seated.

Assegai heads, knives, axes, and so on were forged here, but not hardened. The iron for the forge was obtained from the iron ore in which the district abounds, the refining being done by the blacksmiths themselves. The pieces of iron meant for making assegai blades or such were stuck, after heating in the furnace, into billets of wood for facility in handling. All the implements used were made of hammered iron. A forge such as I have described can be seen at the Pitt Rivers Museum, Oxford. I sent a specimen to Professor Henry Balfour many years ago.

Each night when I camped I had a grass shelter made for sleeping under. They were primitive structures that did not take long to put up, but the point about them was that after retiring the entrance could be closed. This helped to keep off the mosquitoes to some extent, for by the river they were very numerous and assertive.

In the middle of the journey I lost my cook. This

native boy went for a stroll one afternoon. He had not returned by sundown, and when darkness fell I fired a shot or two to recall him, but he did not appear. In the morning search was made. His spoor was found and followed for some distance away from the camp right to the river's edge. There was, however, no sign at all of his returning tracks. There was only one possible verdict: crocodiles.

The loneliness of the trip, the need for sympathetic company, would have been hard to bear if it had not been for my terrier, Flossie. There was no chumming up with the boys, of course, and that jolly little wire-haired lady was my only pal. There was no beating her good humour. She was always the same, and it seemed that there was only one soul in the world she had any use for. That was myself. She clung to my heels, and she was miserable when I was out of her sight.

Sometimes when I went off shooting I would tie her up in camp. My only reason for doing so was that she was much too impetuous. As soon as I fired she would rush forward after the game, as often as not spoiling any chance of a second shot. This, of course, was in the earlier days of our friendship. In time she finished her education and became properly trained. But, leaving her tied up behind me in camp, I would hardly have a mile covered before I would hear a slight noise. And there would be Flossie, paw up, eager, inquiring! Nothing could have kept her in camp but a dog-chain. Rawhide thong or rope could not hold her. She simply gnawed through either in less than no time. Dog-chains were hard to come by within anything but three hundred miles. Perhaps it was as well I could not procure one, because I fancy she discovered the sooner for what fault she was left behind.

Flossie had a marvellous nose. She would follow a wounded buck any distance and she invariably found. I hate to wound an animal and leave it to die. Once I wounded a roan antelope, and it got away. Flossie was after it like a shot. I followed, but at some distance. They disappeared into the bush, and presently I heard barking and made for the sound. When I arrived, Flossie was having a rough time. She was hanging on to the antelope's nostrils, and he was shaking her for all he was worth. He was a big fellow, too, that roan. I dispatched him with a second shot. You may be sure Flossie shared the undercut with me that night.

Once I could have done with the help of Flossie's nose when the retaining cord proved too good for her. I had gone out shooting in the afternoon, and when sundown came I made for my camp. It was after dark when I struck the river, but I had missed my camp entirely. The problem was whether to follow the bank up or down. Either way might have meant getting farther away from my objective. I decided that the best thing to do was to stay put, and I fired the usual shot that would bring some one from camp in search of me. A minute after I had fired one of the boys appeared. The camp, as it happened, was less than a hundred yards away. But it had been made in a hollow, the banks of which prevented me from seeing the fire.

Coming down the river I encountered a Jewish trader going up-country with a cargo of goods. When I came on him he was eating with his native boys, a thing which whites regarded as pretty low down. He complained that he could not get his boys to do anything. They went their own way and would take no notice of anything he said. " They simply laugh at me," he whined. He was nearly crying with self-pity.

" What do you expect when you treat them as equals?" I replied. " It serves you dam' well right!"

This chap lived as a trader in Barotseland for nearly thirty years, and he died there. He had several native wives and a host of pepper-and-salt children. It is hard enough to keep the respect of the natives as things go, but there is nothing lets the white man down so readily as this sort of behaviour.

I learned a lot about the natives on that trip, or at least about handling them. They are as inconsistent as monkeys, and a firm hand is always wanted. One of my troubles with my boat boys came from their habit of landing to make for the bush to collect wild fruit. Sometimes they would be gone for hours. There was little use in protesting, and I couldn't keep a proper eye on more than the boys in my own boat at one time. As a fact, I didn't worry greatly over this trouble. I was in no hurry, and the boys were paid by the journey. They were to be given a five-shilling blanket and three yards of limbo (calico) apiece for the four hundred miles. The fruit-hunting was a minor disobedience. Disobeying direct orders was a different matter, but even on this score I had to assert my authority only twice. I have already told of how I brought the boys up to scratch when they objected to shooting some rapids before dark came on.

The second occasion was at the end of one of the two-day camps I made after shooting a hippo. When I

MY FLEET OF DUG-OUTS

158

wanted to get going again the boys absolutely refused to strike camp or to embark. I ordered them into the boats, and found myself facing rank mutiny. There were sixty of them, armed with assegais, and they seemed to think they had the solitary white man at their mercy. I told them for the last time that if they didn't get a move on with striking camp and loading the boats I would begin shooting. They did not move, so I shot at a branch just above their heads. I had the good luck to bring it down on them. Then I told them that the next shot would be for their leader in mutiny. I meant what I said, too, because the thing had gone beyond bluff if I really meant to keep my end up. Possibly they realized I was in earnest, because they got on with the job immediately. I had no more trouble of that sort on the trip.

In due course, after this leisurely journey, I arrived at at Sesheke, and there I established my headquarters for quite a considerable time.

CHAPTER XII

DIVERS TROUBLES

FROM Sesheke I was to go on another shooting trip. For this I needed to engage a few boats, and I proceeded to interview one Koko, a favourite chief of the King's.

The most I can say for Koko was that he had ' taking ' ways. So taking were his ways, it wasn't safe to leave any portable property unattended in his vicinity. We were bargaining about the boats, he and I, by the river-side, on a steep ten-foot bank, his gang of paddlers with him, when he became grossly impertinent, whereupon I knocked him head over heels into the stream. The place teemed with crocodiles, and Koko was extremely annoyed. So was I, as a matter of fact, but I hired the boats, and Koko came on the trip in person.

On the first afternoon of the expedition we had to shoot some rapids that stretched about a mile. There were three channels through this particular run of rapids, one close to either bank and one in the middle of the river. It was the custom to take either of the bank-side channels in case of accident, but Koko elected to use the centre one. Half-way down the rapids he contrived to upset the dug-out I was travelling in. Fortunately, I could swim like a fish, and I got to the shore quickly without apparent harm.

Next day, however, there were consequences. I developed a terrific bout of fever with a temperature of 104. I was in pretty bad case, I knew, but there was no good in lying around, and I embarked in the morning as usual and made myself as comfortable as I could.

During the afternoon the boats put into an island and we all disembarked. My idea was that the boys were in need of a rest. But Koko, it seemed, was ashore for quite a different purpose. We had gone barely a few yards from the dug-outs when he started shouting and waving an assegai. Then he came straight for me. It was apparent that he had not forgotten the indignity of that ten-foot drop into the river. I let him close, dodged pretty smartly, then slid under his weapon and found a grip. It was no occasion for pretty fighting. I threw him and kicked hell out of him. While he was still wondering whether he was Koko or the middle of next month, I slipped back to the boat and got my trusted ·450. I should never have left it there, of course, but I really was ill.

Koko recovered and got going. He swore he would leave me on the island. I said I wasn't having any—we'd travel in company. He then suggested I should take the boat while he and his boys stopped on the island. "Not at all," I said. "I stop with you whatever you do. If you go on, I'm with you. If you stop here, I stop too. I don't mind stopping. There's plenty of water with the river so handy. I have plenty of skoff. Also lots of baccy."

And here I did about as heroic a thing as I ever did in my life. I was feeling like nothing on earth, with a temperature of 104 still, but to show my unconcern I took out my old briar, filled it, and began smoking. A smoke was the last thing I wanted. It was horrible in my then condition. But for two solid hours I kept it up, and in the end Koko's obstinacy broke. I was requested to get aboard. I was nothing loath. I was glad to get lying down again.

That night we landed on a sandbank, about a hundred and fifty yards long, surrounded by dense reed. I put down my blankets at one end and saw the boys settled at the other. Then I dossed down. I was feverish and wakeful, and in the middle of the night my friend Flossie began to growl. I looked out. A dark figure was crawling on hands and knees towards me, not very far away. I called and asked the fellow what he was after. He said he wanted fire. That was not a very plausible answer, for a fire was going quite well at the other end of the bank. It was plain enough that here was an attempt to knife me. I told the fellow to clear or I would shoot. He cleared.

Not to pad out a situation of a tensity that I can't describe, I will merely say that I had to cut the trip short because of my fever, and there were two further attempts on my life before I got back. Arrived at Sesheke I tied the favourite chief to a tree all night, a proceeding that annoyed him still more, and then turned him over to a newly-imported District Commissioner.

It was somewhat of an effort for me to attend the judicial proceedings at the D.C.'s court, because I was still very seedy. The then paramount chief, my friend Litia, was present, together with two of his brothers.

During the hearing Koko made the admission that he had tried five times to blot me out, but that luck had been against him. The District Commissioner, fresh

FISHING WITH ASSEGAIS

from Oxford, was the sort of fellow who put on a coat to visit the local queen.

"Well," he asked me, "what do you suggest would meet the case?"

"Give him a damned good hiding," said I, "and dock him of his pay."

My suggestion was carelessly lenient, but I was not prepared for what followed.

"This is a very trivial case," the D.C. said. "I shall dock him of his pay."

I am giving you this as an absolute fact. It happened, remember, where white men were few and far between among hordes of blacks. The only explanation I can come to for the D.C.'s action is—funk. The case, however, was reported by the local trader to Mr H. Marshall Hole, the Acting Administrator, and as a result the D.C. was sacked.

After the trial I went to bed for two days. During that time Koko drew his docked pay in kind from my boss boy, pinched the handsome leopard skin given me by Litia, and cleared. Koko, I'll say, was a daisy.

Soon after the fever left me I took on a job with the Government. This was to fetch grain and some bales of blankets from Kasangula. It was a trip of about five days.

The goods at Kasangula were in charge of a Jew, who was camped under a big tree. During the evening of my stay, having nothing much in common to talk about, we fell to playing 'banker.' I lost all I had on me, fortunately no great amount. A week later the Jew followed me to Sesheke, and put up with a fellow Hebrew. To amuse the few white residents, he performed some tricks with playing cards one evening. They were extremely clever tricks; they made me think it small wonder that I had lost at Kasangula! Again I entered the experience to Education Account.

On the way back to Sesheke my flotilla was overtaken by a sudden and heavy storm that threw up high waves. So sudden was the onslaught of the squall that there was no time to land. Five of the dug-outs were sunk, and the remainder were swamped but managed to reach the shore. Fortunately, no lives were lost.

It was on this trip that I secured a fine reed buck while shooting on the flats. I got him running—clean through the heart—at a range of 400 yards. I heard the impact of the bullet as it struck him, but he ran 300 yards before he dropped. I checked this distance by pacing it. My kill had a record pair of horns, twenty-one inches long; it was the only pair of horns I took down-country with me—and thereby hangs a not too pretty tale. The trophy was stolen; I knew very well by whom, but I was a guest of his at the time and could not say a word about the theft. It was a low-down trick, and it prevented the horns being put on record. My ' friend,' of course, didn't dare register the trophy in Rowland Ward's book. He went later to North-eastern Rhodesia, where the horns were seen in his house by people I knew.

When I was skinning the buck, scores of vultures came out of the blue in the expectation of a feed. They settled around within a few yards of me, coming closer and closer each minute. They were enormous fellows, not at all to be scared away. If I shooed them off they merely retreated a couple of paces, then immediately edged in again. I had never seen the like, nor have I since. Unfortunately, I had expended the last film in my camera and could not photograph the scene.

Litia wanted me to remain in Sesheke; he offered me sole trading rights at his brother's place on the Chobe river, but I wanted to be on the move again, and refused. I started for Kasangula and the Old Drift in company with the English trader of Sesheke, who was taking some cash back to the head store at the Old Drift. He had arranged by runner for a couple of horses to be waiting for us at Kasangula.

By this time the rains had started. About five miles below Sesheke my dug-out sprang a leak, so I landed on an island and sent the boat back to be replaced by one that was watertight. My ' half-section ' pushed on, being anxious not to have that large amount of cash on him for longer than he could help, while I had to wait for hours on the island. Close on sundown the new dug-out arrived, and I embarked and set out immediately. It was raining, and I had neither tent, mosquito net, nor food—my trader friend was carrying the lot.

As I passed the mouth of the Kesia river, which ran through my old hunting-ground, the flats, I saw a grand sight. Right on the edge of the bluff was a splendid lion with a magnificent black mane. He was standing with his head up, gazing at the boat. By his side was just as fine a specimen of a lioness.

It became apparent as I went on that I was not to reach Kasangula that night, and I had to camp as best I could on an island. The rain still poured down, and, believe me, it was pretty miserable in the open without tent or mosquito net, particularly the latter. When at times the rain did give over the mosquitoes came round in

165

swarms, humming like a German band. They certainly could sting. I firmly believe they could have penetrated the hide of an elephant. Sleep was out of the question. I was never so glad to see daylight. I was starving. Failing to come up with my trader friend because of that long wait for the replacing dug-out had cooked my goose completely.

It was three o'clock next afternoon before I reached Kasangula. There I found an old white mare waiting to bear me to the Old Drift, but no grub. I saw nothing for it but to push on to Mapondo's kraal and take my chance of obtaining food there. I had not gone very far, however, when a terrific storm of wind and rain sprang up, so violent that the old white mare would not face it. She turned her stern to the tempest, and we had to wait for over an hour under a big tree.

The track was of white sand, overgrown with rank grass. But white sand overgrown with rank grass lay in all directions. Darkness was on us. I realized I had lost the trail. My misery deepened; I was lost, hopeless, and unbearably hungry. The rain still came down, but the violence of the wind had abated. I decided to give the old mare her head. She knew the way to the Old Drift better than I did, I felt, so I dropped the reins and let her head where she damned well chose. I was beyond caring.

The old lady took one deliberate step at a time, and was not in the slightest hurry. I made no move to urge her. She paced steadily on, going at the rate of about two miles an hour, and at three o'clock in the morning I found myself at Mapondo's kraal. I roused some of the natives and asked for food. They were in no particular

NATIVE BLACKSMITHS

hurry, and it seemed an eternity before some Kaffir beans and some thick milk were brought. Then I was shown an empty hut to sleep in. I off-saddled the mare and took the saddle into the hut for use as a pillow. I was still without blankets, but I had got a roof over my head, as I reflected gratefully while listening to the rain, which was still falling with a melancholy persistence. Luckily Flossie was with me, otherwise I should have been lonely indeed.

I tried to sleep, but sleep eluded me. I was being bitten, then I felt a tugging at my hair. What could it be? Suddenly it dawned on me. Tam-pams!

This was my first experience of their attentions; my greatest horror is bugs of any sort, and in bug life tam-pams are Titans, a kind of superbug. I lit out of that hut as if fired from it, taking my saddle with me, and the remainder of the night I tried to sleep in the rain. My saddle got soaked through, and so did I. At dawn I arose, saddled the mare, and set out on the last stage of the journey. The wet saddle did not give the mare a sore back, but it about flayed me, and I rode the last few miles without connecting with the saddle. It was days before I could sit in comfort. I arrived at the Old Drift just after lunch was over at Mopani's hotel, and all I could get to eat was a hunk of bread and a tin of Vienna sausages. But I was far from particular, and just then anything eatable would have been a feast. After the meal a hut was provided for me, and I needed no rocking into the long, long sleep that ensued. I was completely done up.

I made my headquarters at the Old Drift for the time

being, but my intention was to settle at Victoria Falls as soon as the railway was completed, for I believed that there would be great opportunities for those who got in early at the railhead. At the end of the year I engaged a man to build a hut for me near the spot where the railway station would be pitched, and where the hotel would be built, but I had no mind to cross the river until the railway did come up.

Dr Wilson, an old hand whom I knew very well in Bulawayo, and who had settled at the Old Drift three months before I started north, died of blackwater fever just before I got back there. During the rainy season, which continued from November to March, the place was a swamp; out of the thirty-one settlers there, no less than eleven died of blackwater fever or malaria that winter. Surely a high percentage, that. The Old Drift was, none the less, a real cheery camp and the settlers were good fellows.

There was a funeral about once every week. When a settler died one of the others was elected as undertaker, and had to make a coffin out of old whisky cases. This when knocked together was finished off with a covering of black limbo, or calico. When the departed had been encased, the coffin was placed on a Scotch cart drawn by oxen and was hauled to the burial ground. Everybody in the settlement walked behind, clad in ordinary attire, slacks and shirts, no coats, and with shirt-sleeves rolled up to the elbow. When the grave was reached the coffin would be lowered into it. We had no Bibles or Prayer Books in the camp, so somebody would recite what he remembered of the Burial Service, and the others would prompt or carry on to the best of their ability.

168

Once when a coffin was being lowered into the grave it stuck half-way down. The grave hadn't been made wide enough. The 'undertaker,' leaning forward to see what was the matter, overbalanced and fell in on top of the coffin. We hoisted him up, and the coffin after him, and then the grave had to be widened to get this particular parishioner decently planted. Usually after the grave was filled in we went off to have a drink, asking each other sadly, " Wonder who'll be the next? "

The rainy season following also took its toll of the Old Drifters. At its end seventy per cent. of the settlers had paid in their checks. Just think of that! Seventy per cent.! Pioneering wasn't all lavender.

I was not, myself, at the Old Drift during that second rainy season. The railway had come along and I had migrated to the Falls. Still, I had several months there, during which I was subject to fever regularly. As a fact, like the rest, I was never really quit of it.

At that time on the Drift my great pal was an engineer called Billy, of whom I have a story to tell by and by. But for the moment I want to tell how Billy got the fever out of me in remarkable and drastic fashion. For six consecutive weeks I had been having fever on and off— one day feeling bad, next day feeling rotten, and the next better. When the seventh dose was coming on I got the shakes as usual and retired to bed. But day after day went by and I simply could not get a sweat to break out. At long last Billy conceived a bright idea for inducing that saving perspiration, and he asked me if I was game to try it.

" I'll jolly well kill or cure you," says he. " What about it? "

" I don't give a damn what happens," I replied. " Have a go."

Billy got everything ready, and I stripped. My friend had a spirit kettle and a large native stool made out of a solid block of wood. This had a large hole in the bottom, and it was turned upside down for me to sit on it. Billy filled the kettle with water and lit the lamp under it, then made a blanket tent about me from head to foot. The kettle soon boiled—and so did I. I made a few trenchant remarks and wanted to move, but I was helpless and it was easy to hold me down. For ten minutes I was steamed. A few carrots and parsnips steamed with me would have made a meal for anyone, and not parrot food either. But I sweated. Indeed I sweated.

When the process finished I was scarlet from head to heel. I was then rolled in blankets and put to bed, where I glided off into heavenly dreams while Billy read aloud from a technical book on bridge-building—being an engineer from birth. He seemed annoyed because I kept falling asleep.

One fine afternoon Billy, Flossie, and I took it into our heads to have a bit of fishing. We set out in a Canadian canoe with five native paddlers. About half a mile above the Old Drift Billy espied a young crocodile that was just showing its head above water and decided to give it ' one for its nob.' Seizing a paddle he commanded the boys to glide quietly alongside it. The croc was about thirty yards off the shore, and when he got into what he considered striking distance Billy launched a terrific swipe at it. In a flash the croc went under; in the same flash the canoe heeled clean over and we were

MY SLEEPING-SHELTER

all in the water. Before one could say 'Knife!' the native boys were on the bank, and I was a good second behind them.

There was a yell behind me:

" For God's sake, Clark—lend me a hand! I'm drowning! "

I came about, and there was Billy still struggling a yard away from the boat.

" Get back to the boat, Billy! " I shouted. " I'm coming! "

He managed to reach the canoe, but it was nearly awash. He grabbed its side on the beam, and, of course, his weight made it turn over and over, he with it. Billy lost his head completely then and went into a panic. I reached the canoe and steadied it from one end, and yelled to Billy to get to the other.

But Billy was too excited to do anything so sensible. I cussed him like a trooper, explaining the worthlessness of his pedigree in five different languages, including good old Anglo-Saxon. That seemed to steady him. He contrived to get to the stern of the canoe, and I pushed him ashore.

I will admit that all the time I was pushing I was in no small funk. I could not help imagining how many of the young croc's immediate relations and for-bears might be handy, and of the unpleasant compli-cations that might arise. Flossie stuck by me during all these manœuvres, and I fancy enjoyed the fun. I was wearing a stiff-brimmed Baden-Powell hat, and Flossie was perched on it during some of the performance.

The following day I went back to the same spot with a gun and managed to bag the young croc. It was about three feet long. Stuffed, he ornaments a room in the Old Country to-day.

The crowd at the Old Drift about this time might have been called cosmopolitan. The original settler was Mopani Clarke, who ran a store and hotel. He also acted as forwarding agent for the Northern Copper Company. A chemist came up with Dr Wilson, but he soon had enough of it and went south when Dr Wilson died. Van Blerk ran a store for a Bulawayo firm, and Tom King ran another and a canteen for the Bechuanaland Trading Company. Another fellow, Dipper by name, had a mineral-water plant. Then there was Billy, my engineer friend and one or two store assistants. Another chap we called ' Yank ' hung around. What his business actually was we couldn't say, but he certainly was very lucky at poker. He had got as far as beginning to build a hut for himself, and he had collected a lot of grass for thatching it. One day he offered to sell this grass to me, and I bought it at threepence a bundle to use as roofing for my hut at the Victoria Falls. I wondered why he sold the stuff to me, but two or three nights after the transaction he disappeared and was never heard of again. I fancy his phenomenal luck at cards had something to do with it, and that he was advised to clear out.

One Sunday morning some five or six of the crowd were having a ' usual ' or two. One or other of us was seated on the bar counter, others were lounging here and there. A couple perhaps were seated on empty whisky cases. Certainly a pair were at the far end of the counter rolling poker dice. Into the midst of this choice Sunday

REED BUCK SHOT BY THE AUTHOR

morning assembly there came a stranger with a week's beard on his chin. His clothes were ragged, and his boots beyond repair.

"Have a drink?" one of the crush suggested hospitably.

"No, thanks. I don't drink," the stranger replied. "But I would like to hold a service here."

There was a moment's silence, then somebody spoke up.

"Well," he said. "We don't mind trying anything once. Let's give it a whirl, boys."

I was elected to the chair for the meeting, and after we had filled up again the service was begun. Our teetotal friend started off with a hymn, and everybody contributed a row that might, with a stretch of imagination, have been called singing. Some could sing, some couldn't, but the noise ended with Joe in the lead by a short head.

After that came prayer and a hymn or two more, then I was asked to address the meeting.

"*Ikona!*" said I. "Nothing doing!"

"But I am sure you are a good man," the visitor remarked.

"You're a liar!" said I, taken aback. "Get ahead with it yourself."

This he proceeded to do like a real professional. The service came to an end and I took round the hat. The takings ran to a good feed for the preacher, a new pair of boots, and a couple of quid to stick in his pocket—which wasn't such a bad collection from half a dozen or so hard cases.

This was the first service held at the Old Drift.

While I lived at the Old Drift I spent a lot of my

time at the Victoria Falls taking photographs, and I got together quite a good collection. I would camp out for a couple of days at a time in the hut that was building for me. When that was completed I lived in it, but for most of the time I was over on the other side at the Old Drift. I liked the older haunts, and the old crowd.

CHAPTER XIII

THE OLD DRIFT

IN those days of the Old Drift the mail was supposed to run once a week. Zeederberg was contractor for the mail, and he used to bring it from the railhead in a Scotch cart drawn by mules or oxen. In the rainy season I have known his Majesty's mails to be three weeks late from being unable to get across flooded rivers.

The arrival of the mail at the Drift was announced by a bugle-call, and, whatever might be doing day or night, the whole of the inhabitants would troop down to the north bank. A dug-out or canoe would be sent across the river, and the bags brought back to a hut that served as temporary post-office. The mail would be emptied out of the bags on the hut floor, and every one took a hand in sorting it out. There was, of course, much excitement in the process, with everybody hoping for letters from home, whether in South Africa or the Old Country. It was the great event of the week. The actual post-office was on the sand belt five miles away, but the Postmaster rode in from there to receive or deliver the mails.

All the inhabitants were wont to meet each night at one or other of the settlement's two bars, for these were the only clubs we had. It should be remembered that there were no real homes in the camp—merely places for sleeping in, huts or tents. No women were there to bring any refining influence. And the men, in their gregariousness, collected of course where recreation, such as it was, was to be had.

The first woman, I think, to appear at the settlement was brought along by one of the traders. He said she was his wife, and she was always addressed by his name.

The trader, a Dutchman, was extremely jealous, and showed it plainly if anyone made a fuss of the dame or spent too much time in her company. He often had to go off on visits to his cattle posts, and in his absence there were certainly ' bees around the honey-pot.' There was one fellow, however, whom she made a particular favourite, and in the trader's absence this fellow spent most of his time with her. The trader came to hear of it. A very hefty specimen, he was very wild about it, and he went about stopping further intrigues of the sort in vigorous fashion. As a Dutchman he was expert in the use of the sjambok, the whip made of hippo hide, and one night, with another Dutchman of the same size as himself, he went to the hut of the Lothario. This hut stood alone on the bank of the river. The two Dutchmen broke in, and while the second held the offender down the trader thrashed him unmercifully, even over the face, until he was hardly recognizable. I saw the man next day. He was terribly disfigured.

The man was English, which meant, of course, that he was not going to take a thrashing of that sort quietly. As soon as he could move he went round the camp hunting for any sort of gun with which to shoot the trader. He was mad with rage. Nobody, of course, had a gun to lend him. One fellow, however, was too slow, and

ON THE BANKS OF THE ZAMBESI

had a Martini on view when the would-be borrower turned up. There was a struggle for the weapon, but the Englishman was weak from the thrashing, and on the short side anyhow, and he was defeated of his purpose. If he had managed to get away with that rifle it is certain that there would have been two deaths in the camp that night. I knew the man particularly well; he was just the fellow in the first incidence of his rage and humiliation to have bumped off the Dutchman. He did send an order to Bulawayo for a Browning pistol, but I suppose by the time it arrived wiser counsel had had effect and he saw that his neck was of more value to him than revenge.

I remember vividly the day when ' It '—as we called him—arrived on the mail cart. ' It ' was a regular Ha-ha Johnnie, with a ' Piccadilly window ' in his eye. Installed in Mopani's Rest House, he informed the world that he had come to " shoot a bally lion." His boots were chalked according to custom, and he was given the Freedom of the City, but his leg was pulled unmercifully.

After asking all sorts of dam'-fool questions, he put the query: Where was the best place to shoot a lion? One of the old-timers advocated shooting it in the groin and then cutting its throat with a safety razor. Another fetched out the ancient suggestion of putting salt on its tail and finishing it off with a pea-shooter.

" I don't mean that, you bally asses," our visitor said blandly. " I mean—where's the best place to *go* to shoot a lion? "

That, of course, gave us our chance. He promptly was given directions which would take him to a spot where

M   177

AUTOBIOGRAPHY OF AN OLD DRIFTER

no lion had ever been seen or heard of, and we started him off at ten in the morning, under a broiling hot sun, to shoot his ' bally lion.' He returned in time for lunch—goat and wild spinach—and sank into a chair, worn and weary.

" Any luck, old man? "

The question was put with a great show of interest and a sideways wink.

" Yaas, certainly," was the amazing reply. " You fellows put me on to a very good place indeed. Couldn't have been better, in fact. I shot a bally lion."

And, as it turned out—*he bally-well had!*

But there it is, you know—' a fool for luck! ' Johnny was one up on me, at least, for I had been among lions and had sought them, but had never shot one.

We were something wild and woolly, we Old Drifters, in the early days. There was Jimmy, for example. He was a hippo hunter. He used to go up-river for sixty miles to Kasangula, then trek up the Chobe river. The hippo hides that he collected he cut into strips and brought down-country to sell for sjamboks and so on ; they fetched good prices and he made money at the game. A hard case if ever there was one, Jimmy was an ex-cowboy from the States. He was tough and had a face like a gargoyle, and he bristled with guns, knives, and ammunition. With either rifle or revolver he was a dead shot.

Whenever Jimmy had ' one over the eight ' he came all over pathetic and would recite *Over the Hills to the Poorhouse*, his favourite set of verses. By the time he got to the end he was weeping copiously. I remember once when Jimmy, myself, and another fellow were having a quiet one—Jimmy seated in his most usual position, cross-legged on the bar counter—some one came in with a message.

" Have a drink, Sporty," Jimmy invited.

" No, thanks."

" Have a drink, Sporty! " Jimmy repeated with a certain sort of emphasis.

" No, thanks! "

" *Have a drink, Sporty!* " And *bang-bang-bang*! went Jimmy's revolver, with the shots all about Sporty's feet.

" Yes, please," said Sporty. But I don't think I'd have let Jimmy have his will with me in that fashion.

Jimmy was in the habit of hiring carriers for the two-hundred-mile trip from the Chobe river to the Drift, giving them two shillings a head to bear a load of hippo-hide strips. A couple of years after the time I'm telling of one of my friends went hippo hunting on the Chobe. Being in need of carriers for the journey back, he got in touch with some natives who had carried for Jimmy and offered them five shillings a head for bringing his loads into the Drift. The offer was very definitely refused. " No," said the natives. " We want the same as Boss Jimmy gives us—two shillings each! "

The following, by permission, is quoted from the Christmas Number of the *Livingstone Mail* for 1908. It appeared under the heading, " The Chronicles of Deadrock." ' Deadrock,' to the initiated, meant the Old Drift. I think it gives a fair description of an evening there:

Even Yank did not call Deadrock a ' city.' It is not even a village. It is merely a trading post on the Zambesi, situated

179

near the only drift it has for miles; and a good proportion of the goods and passenger trade—even as far as the Lakes—must cross there. Nemesis in the form of a huge railway bridge threatens it with extinction in the near future, and Deadrock, which has now attained the dignity of a place on the map, will be swallowed up in swamp again, and ' Ichabod ' shall be writ upon the hearts of the people.

The principal feature of Deadrock is the mosquito. He is the true anophele, energetic and indiscriminating; the loafer and the lord on a hunting expedition are treated with strict impartiality—for the mosquito is a democrat, and cursed is he who forgetteth his quinine o' nights, for the shakes and the vomiting shall surely affect him.

Some half-dozen wood and iron stores, and twice as many wattle and daub Kaffir stores, comprise the settlement The larger stores are also hotels and have bars attached to them, where you shall see the inhabitants of Deadrock; for the heat is an oppressive heat and the thirst engendered thereby requireth sedulous and unintermittent slaking. There was a time when customs duties were rebated, and the old hands still speak, with a reminiscent glow, of the time when a whisky and soda was only a shilling.

There are only two hours in Deadrock—sunrise and sunset; so that eleven o'clock is a movable feast and, as a matter of fact, often sets in before breakfast. But it is at night that the bar—for it is a feature that only one bar is patronized on a particular night; the other two may close up—attains to its full glory and splendour. A gramophone sings: " I may be crazy, but I love you—tiddley-um-tum-tum! " in one corner. In another, half a dozen merchants and speculators are throwing poker dice over the counter for drinks. In a third, a roulette table is in full swing, while in a fourth some one with last night's winnings in his pockets is drawing a faro bank. " Deuce to an ace and nobody hurt," says the banker, " leave that in hock." " Don't touch it or you'll burn your darn fingers." " Now then, gentlemen—all ready? And its ten to a trey—durn that trey! That's the fo'th time you've brought off a parole—is that two quid on the nine-six or the ten-five? Will you put it on the corner? Pay the ace-ten?—with pleasure, sir! Now are you all ready?" "Zero's turned up twice running," says some one, and all glance at the roulette table where the imperturbable croupier is raking in the chips, and filling up a column of thirty half-crowns—the reward of some punter who has probably lost twice as much on the red.

"Round and round the little ball goes, and where she stops there's nobody knows! Put it down, gentlemen! No seed, no harvest—if you don't speculate, you can't accumulate—and she's off! Hands off the lay-out!" A moment's silence while the ball spins. "It's sixteen and a red, first column" (pronounced 'colume') "—second twelve and even—change for a five? Just wait half a minute till I'm through paying." "What's yours, sir?" "Whisky and ginger ale." "How much are these?" queries a newcomer, pointing to the white chips. "Shilling each," says the croupier. "And the reds?" "Five shillings." "They're dam' dear—but—well, give us a quid's worth." And so it goes on. The stakes are fairly high, but not relatively so. In Deadrock a shilling is nothing worth. You can't get your hair cut under half-a-crown—and what a cut! A hundred-pound faro bank has been broken in half an hour, and a second for the same amount has lasted very little longer. In the long run, however, the only safe and sure winner is the bar, for the banker is perpetually adjured to stand the drinks, and even a lucky punter will find himself called on for a round now and then.

It must not be assumed, however, that faro and roulette are the only games played. Vingt-et-un breaks out now and then, and there is a steady school of inveterate gamblers who play a 'compulsory four-blind' game of poker every night, including Sundays.

Other social life there is none. A postprandial lying contest, chiefly concerned with niggers and lions, may take place now and then, or a party be made up to go hippo hunting. There are no societies or dance committees, and there probably isn't a dress suit in the camp.

This, as I have said, is a very fair description of life at the Old Drift, written by myself at the time.

After the evening's recreation was over, many of us

would troop into the store for a feed before retiring. Tinned prawns, sardines, and canned goods of the kind, with hard biscuits composed the menu. The yapping would go on for half an hour or so, then all would retire.

Even at the Old Drift we had our weekly paper, *The Livingstone Pioneer*. The editor and proprietor was the local chemist. It was typewritten and reproduced in quantity by one of those gelatine gadgets with which you get a printing by sticking the sheets on a gummy slab and running a roller over them. It was a very popular weekly with an enormous circulation—sometimes as many as fifty copies a week net sales. I still have several copies in my possession, and find it interesting from time to time to re-read them.

The successor to the *Pioneer* was *The Livingstone Mail*. It was owned and run by the same man, and it too was typewritten. I have a copy of the first issue—which is more than its editor can say. The office file was destroyed by white ants. The paper is still going strong under the same editor and proprietor, but in these days it comes off real printing presses. The editor, Mr L. F. Moore, a well-known figure in politics, has offered me a guinea for my copy of the first issue—an offer which I consider mere trifling.

Some of the first Christmas Numbers were remarkable efforts. The covers, I believe, were produced in the Old Country. They enfolded some sixteen pages in 1908, with two inside pages of illustrations. They were coloured covers. Under a red band showing the title, *The Livingstone Mail*, in white, were five half-tone cuts of " A Native Band," " The Club House," " Tobacco

Plantation," "Administrator's Punt on the Zambesi," and "A View of the Falls," all against a decoration of bluish leaves. The legend ran in red: "Christmas Number. Price 2s." For an up-country production it was a distinctly good effort.

Fever was so prevalent at the Old Drift that we took it almost as a matter of course. No particular attention was given to anyone down with it. As a rule, only one's personal native servant would be in attendance if one was sick, though, of course, anyone who happened to be passing and had a few minutes to spare would drop in and do what he could for the patient.

Our chemist disappeared one day. He had been delirious for some time. For over a week he was lost— then he was found dead in the bush two or three miles out from the settlement, his body in a dreadful state of putrefaction. The undertaker got very drunk before facing the job of bringing it in; none envied him the job, notwithstanding a plentiful supply of quick-lime. The chemist was buried at midnight by the light of torches, and when lowered into the grave the coffin also was covered with chloride of lime. This was the second occasion when I was present that the undertaker fell into the grave; this time it was because he was tight. Joe was so tight, in fact, that in spite of the chloride of lime he refused to shift from the top of the coffin, and had to be hauled out by main force. There was some excuse, of course, for Joe's getting drunk.

There were, however, several men who frequently took too much liquor without any excuse at all. Jimmy, the hippo hunter, was a case in point. Out in the veldt he never touched a drop, but when he got back to camp he developed an apparently unquenchable thirst. He kept it going from six in the morning till six in the morning, with very short intervals for repose. Naturally, he saw things—red, white, and blue, and striped—and being such a crack with the revolver he spent a lot of time shooting them as they ran about the roof timbers of his hut. In course of time the roof of the hut was like a colander for holes that perhaps gave extra ventilation but let in too much of the rain. In later years my wife and myself tried hard to reform him, but without success. In camp he simply couldn't leave hard liquor alone.

Another fellow who 'got 'em' was 'Taffy.' He got 'em so badly one night that he ran from the Old Drift, clad only in his nightshirt and with nothing on his feet, to the Magistrate's house on the sand belt four miles away. He swore he was chased by snakes and other vermin of all hues the whole of the way.

The village policeman whom the Government ultimately allotted to us was also a bit of a hard case. He took his duties very lightly, worrying nobody and nobody worrying at all about him. He took part in all the fun that was going. He possessed only two shirts, and when he felt that he was getting tight he used to change out of his newer shirt into the older one. He realized how much he enjoyed a scrap when half-cut, and he didn't want the better shirt to get damaged. Water was cooled in a big canvas bag that somewhat resembled a punch-ball. This was suspended from the bar ceiling close to the wall. One night our policeman took it into his head that exercise with the punching ball was just what he needed. Steadying himself to get a good punch in for a start, he let drive with a beauty. But he must have been seeing two punch-balls and have hit the wrong one, for the punch landed on the panel of the door. He left us to go on leave, but he had been home only two days when he died of blackwater fever. Then we heard that our policeman was a Baronet.

It was not everybody that succeeded at the Old Drift. We had our failures. One enterprising fellow started a cotton-gin, but there was no cotton to keep the gin going and his venture failed. He was too proud to ask help from anyone, and he literally starved to death. This does not reflect on the good-heartedness of the Old Drifters. They would have grub-staked anybody, but they simply did not know the man was without resources.

Another resident had a hard struggle. He was a black-smith, and had a wife and family to keep. He mended wagons, but there were few in the district, and his work on those wagons that he did mend was not, I'm afraid, always paid for. The chief diet for himself and family was mealie pap, supplemented by fish that he caught in the river. The smith was a very fine chap, but he had pitched on the wrong spot to set up his smithy, for there really was little transport from the Old Drift.

I have earlier mentioned the other Clarke at the Old Drift, referring to him once or twice as the original settler and as ' Mopani,' who ran the hotel and store. He had some cattle on the other side of the river, which were not allowed to cross. These were in the charge of a piccaninny, who came across once a week to draw his rations. One week this piccanin' said he was afraid to stop among the cattle because there were lots of lions about, and he was promised relief. The next week he

185

did not turn up for his rations as usual. Two of the storemen went across the river to see if the boy and the cattle were all right. At first they could find no trace of the lad, but ultimately came on some rags that they could identify as his clothing. Then four hundred yards from these they came on what was left of him—his skull, one foot, and a few more remnants of clothing. The lions had got him.

Apropos of lions, I might as well tell a couple of stories about them, although the incidents come later chronologically.

One of my friends went out for a day's shooting. At night, when he was sleeping in his tent, the flaps of which were open, he felt a tug at his *kaross*, or blanket of skins. It was being pulled slowly off his bed. Against the light of the tent opening he made out the form of an animal which he took to be a jackal. He picked up his rifle, which lay alongside his bed, and let the beast have it as it moved out of the tent. My friend, satisfied with scaring off the intruder, then turned over and went to sleep again without thinking any more about the incident. Next morning, however, when he got out of his tent, he saw the corpse of the beast he had shot lying not many yards away. It was a lion.

There was a Greek with us at the Old Drift who made his living by shooting meat for the camp. He was out at dawn one misty morning, and he got on top of an ant-hill—they are often as much as twelve feet high—to survey the country. Close at hand he saw what he took to be eleven wild pig. Now, these make good eating when not too old, and he fired at them, one after the other. Out of the eleven he bagged nine, but on going to collect the bag he found he had killed nine lions. This is not the only instance of the kind I know, for lions have often been mistaken for wild boar. " If I had known they was lions," said the Greek later on, " I'd have run like 'ell! "

CHAPTER XIV

THE GORGE OF THE FALLS

IN the New Year of 1904, Charles Beresford Fox, nephew of the designer of the Victoria Falls bridge, Sir Douglas Fox, arrived on the southern bank to begin operations on the foundations for the bridge. Five white men and a large number of natives started to work on getting down to solid rock at the site half-way down the gorge below the Falls.

I got into the way of stopping with Fox at his camp, and in his spare time we wandered about a good deal together, exploring and taking photographs. One day we determined to descend to the bottom of the gorge. It was a descent that had not been done from the southern side by anyone previously, a fact which whetted our eagerness to pull it off. We started from the point where the work on the foundations had been begun, using the ladders that went down to the base of the working.

From here we clambered along the face of the gorge wall, looking for some place that might afford a relatively easy descent the rest of the way. The way, however, that we finally did choose was not to be easy. It was, indeed, perilous going, with thick and thorny undergrowth, but eventually we got down to within twenty feet or so of the bottom. Thereafter came a sheer drop, which we successfully negotiated by tying the rope we had with us to a tree and sliding down. So far, so good. We were actually the first to get to the bottom of this wonderful gorge from the southern bank.

Arrived at the bottom the going was extremely difficult. It was all huge rocks, detached from one another, and about the size, generally, of houses. But we worked towards the neck of the gorge, and came at last to a place where there was no way of making further progress except along a very narrow ledge. To me the risk of attempting the ledge seemed too big for what it was worth. One slip meant a fall into the rushing torrent below, with not the slightest hope of recovery. I refused to chance it. But Fox, always a reckless sort of Johnny, went over, and I made my way back to explore in the opposite direction.

I did not think it wise to remain in the gorge after sun-down, and after a while I thought it time to return. Now, the men working on the opposite side of the gorge had a habit of doing all their blasting at the end of their day's operations. It was plain that they had not seen me on the gorge bottom, for as I clambered back to where we had left the rope a whole lot of charges went off with a terrific uproar, throwing tremendous rocks in all directions about the gorge. One huge piece that looked to me to be as big as a hut came sailing over as if to land on my head. I threw up my arm to ward it off. It landed, however, about fifty yards from me with a terrific crash. My relief was immense, for I had thought my last day was come.

There was no sign of Fox. I shinned up the rope and began the climb to the top. Half-way up I sat down for a rest, when it occurred to me that Fox could not have returned or I should have seen him; it was clear that I must go back and look for him. So once again I descended.

When I regained the bottom and had worked along a bit I saw a workman on the other side of the gorge making urgent signals to me. He seemed to be directing me to proceed along the gorge and up its side. My interpretation was that Fox had come to a point where he thought he could get out of the gorge another way, but had stuck. I hastened on and came to the ledge which I had baulked at crossing earlier. There was no stopping me this time, for I was uneasy about the possible plight of my friend, so I took off my boots as a precaution against slipping, and made the passage. Soon I came to a sort of mound about 150 feet high which I thought Fox had probably gone up. For two solid hours I kept trying to get to the top of this mound, first from one side and then from the other, but from each point I attempted I could get no higher than perhaps about a quarter of the way.

It was becoming dusk, and I thought there was nothing for it but to go back by the way I had come and get help from the workmen's camp. I again safely negotiated the ledge and reached the hanging rope. There was no great length of rope to climb, but I failed in several attempts to get over the top of the rock. I was too exhausted. Willy-nilly I must spend the night in the gorge. I tied myself on to a ledge and settled down. My bed was a wet one, for water condensed from the spray fell on me in rivulets.

It was weird beyond description to be lying thus in the darkness. It was as if spirits of the mist floated around me, moaning and whining. Here a faint sibilant whisper, there the deep groan wrenched from a lost soul. The roar of the tremendous cataract would swell to thunder, and die again to a whisper. I have often noticed since, and wondered, how at full flood the deep roaring of the Falls will seem to break off into sudden silence. At times this sudden apparent silence is as impressive as a thunderclap out of a clear sky.

As I lay there I kept wishing that I had some whisky to go with the spray. Dawn broke at last, and once again I essayed to climb the rope. This time I managed it, and clambered to the top of the gorge. There I found Flossie waiting for me. My little pal had not moved from the spot where I had left her the previous afternoon.

I staggered the half mile or so to the men's camp and found them at breakfast. " Where's Fox? " I asked. " We've got him," they said. " Where's the whisky? " was my next question, and they gave me a stiff tot. I will say that I needed it. Then I had some breakfast, and one of the men, who had been a medical student, came with me to Fox's camp. I was told that a doctor had been sent for by runner to Wankie, a hundred miles away. I asked what had happened.

Fox had got to the top of the mound which I failed to climb, but had been unable to get down again. Nor could he climb up from it. His shouts had been heard by the workmen before they knocked off work for the day, and they had gone along and lowered a rope to him. Instead of tying himself to it and letting them haul him up, he had started to climb it hand over hand. Towards the top the rope was slippery with mud from the spray and damp earth; his hands slipped and he fell about a hundred feet, but had a miraculous escape from death. Fortunately he landed on the branch of a tree, and toppled from that on to a ledge of rock. No bones were broken, but he had an awful shock, from which I believe he never really recovered. A crane was erected, but with every effort on the part of the men they could not get him to the top until four o'clock in the morning. In the meantime I had been reported dead and missing, and somebody had already departed south to Bulawayo with the news.

The quondam medical student who came with me from the men's camp was going to look after Fox, and my idea was to have a rest. But when we got to Fox's camp we found he had regained consciousness, and my companion prescribed rubbing him down with oil. I bore a hand with the treatment, and we got Fox well rubbed down as far as the front of him was concerned. Then we had to turn him over. I took his head and Pat, the medico, his feet. Before we had got him half-turned over I fell right across Fox's face, nearly smothering him. I was out on my feet, fast asleep. I was put to bed and I slept the clock round.

And that, if it please you, is the history of the first known descent into the gorge below the Victoria Falls from the southern side.

Fox was the first man to cross the gorge. Before the bridging of the ravine if one wanted to get from one end of the Falls to the other one had to make a journey of eight miles. That is, one had to go up the river above the Falls, cross to the other side, then come back down-river again. To-day it is a matter of two hundred yards.

FOX CROSSING THE GORGE

To establish communication from one side to the other a rocket with a thin string attached to it was fired across the gorge. On the first trial this was a failure, the rocket falling short. The second shot succeeded, the twine took over a thicker cord, then, finally, a steel cable was hauled across. To this eventually was hooked a bo'sun's chair for conveying passengers from side to side. The crossing normally took about ten minutes, the cable being operated by winding on a winch—a slow business. Sometimes the cable worked off the winch; it was so heavy that it took some time to be wound back again. The first time I went over the crossing took half an hour. Seated on a small plank like the seat of a child's swing and with my legs in a sack I was very much aware of the tumult and surge of the torrent 400 feet below, and I felt anything but happy. It was a trial to the strongest nerves to be suspended, with only a rope to cling to, above those boiling rapids. I was the fourth man to cross the gorge.

It was not until a bag containing the mails was jerked off the hook into the gorge that it dawned on the engineer in charge that the crossing had its dangers. The bag, of course, was light compared with a man, and so was the more readily jerked off. After this accident the hook on the cable was provided with a safety catch which prevented the loop of any burden working off it.

Controversy was great at the bridge camps and the Old Drift as to whether or not there were fish in the gorge. There were those who said they had seen what looked like fish from the top. It was a controversy that interested me, and I made up my mind to try to settle it. A fortnight after my night at the gorge bottom I made a second descent. This time I took my native servant with me and some stout fishing-tackle. This consisted of thin rope borrowed from the bridge works. Attached to it were three great shark-hooks bound with wire, much in the manner of those attached to spoon bait in trolling for pike or tiger fish. I put a large chunk of raw meat on each of the hooks, and slung the line out into the rushing waters of the gorge. Presently the line ran out and I hauled in a fish about four feet long. It looked like a cross between an eel and a barbel, with a softish fin running right along its back and down its belly.

The second cast resulted in what appeared to be a catch-up on a rock. My boy and I put our combined weight on the line to pull it free. For a time it seemed to be stuck for good; then suddenly it gave. We hauled in, and a huge head, as big as a human being's, appeared on the surface. It was like a gargoyle. We put all our weight on the line but failed to haul the monster in. At length we wound the line round a large rock, trusting to the stoutness of the line and the strength of the hooks to prevent Leviathan from getting away. But suddenly there was a terrific jerk, and the brute was gone. And in going, as we saw when we pulled in the line, it had straightened the two hooks it had taken into its mouth. I am quite convinced there are enormous fish in the gorge!

I skinned the barbel-eel, intending to send it to the British Museum. But a Bulawayo man who was on a visit to the Falls suggested that, as a Rhodesian, I ought rather to send it to the Bulawayo Museum. He offered to take the fish to Bulawayo himself and I agreed. Some time later I received a letter from the curator of the museum, who said that the fish was of a new unclassified species and that further information would be sent on. A few months later I had occasion to go to Bulawayo, and naturally I went to see how my capture looked in the museum. There had been some sort of spring-cleaning there, and specimens were lying around in heaps. Of my fish, however, there was no trace, and no trace of it has been found to this day.

I have always regretted that I did not keep to my first intention of sending the fish to the British Museum. It was, after all, the first fish to be taken out of the gorge below the Victoria Falls, and I feel sure the B.M. would have been more interested and have taken better care of this example of an interesting new species.

The report of my death—like Mark Twain's, " grossly exaggerated "—had some odd sequels. There was a very decent sort called Percy Wild, who was a book-keeper at the Bechuanaland Trading Association's store. Soon after I got back to the Old Drift from the bridge camp I ran into him.

" What did you say, Percy," I asked, " when you heard that I was dead? "

" I said, ' Poor old blighter! '—and went and had a drink," he replied.

" That's not a bad idea," I said to him. " Let's have one now."

And we did. A few weeks later Percy was dying. All day long I sat by his bedside, feeding him with champagne with a feather. Outside, in the evening, the lads of the village were sitting under the old sausage tree

195

waiting for news. About eight o'clock Percy passed over, and I went out.

"How's Percy?—how's Percy?" the inquiry went round the fever-stricken group.

"Gone," I told them.

"Poor old blighter!" they said. "Let's go and have a drink!"

About this time I heard from an old friend, Colin Lunn, with whom I had lived in Norwich before coming out to Africa, telling that he was on his way to Rhodesia. Since it was on my urging that he was coming, I thought it only proper that I should go down to Bulawayo and give him a welcome on arrival.

For three days it had been raining. I had to get to Matetsi, the rail-head at the time, to catch a construction train. Four miles below the Falls was the Matsui river. When I came to it I found it in flood, with a group of natives on either side waiting to cross. Some of them had been waiting for two days, but there was no hope of the river dropping in level until the rain ceased. I was in a hurry. I might have to wait days for the water to go down. I stripped and, carrying my clothes in a bundle on my head, began to wade. The natives tried all they could to dissuade me, but I was determined. The river was not very wide, and I thought I could manage it. I got in to the depth of my shoulders, when I found myself going downstream with the tips of my toes just touching the bottom. A mile farther down, the river fell into the gorge of the Zambesi in a three-hundred-foot drop. If I failed to make the opposite bank now, I was a goner for a certainty. And a goner I would have been had the natives on the other side not made a hand-

THE BRIDGE DURING CONSTRUCTION

196

to-hand chain of themselves and swung out to help me. They caught me all right and I landed safely on the southern bank.

I had a long walk after that to the rail-head, but I got there in time to catch the south-bound train. There were no carriages attached to it, and I had to travel in an open ballast truck—for which accommodation I paid a shilling a mile. It was anything but a comfortable trip, unbearably hot when the sun came out, and I was happy when it ended and I found myself in Bulawayo once again.

I met my friend and he was glad to see me after his long journey. When I sent for him to come out to Africa I had a job fixed. But for reasons that I needn't go into he could not get away in time, and the post was filled when he arrived. I established him, however, in another, and he settled down bravely in Bulawayo to get himself a living.

I stopped only a few days in Bulawayo, and a lot of fun was poked at me in the Club over my reported death in the gorge. On the night before I left I was run to ground by a reporter of the *Bulawayo Chronicle*, who had been trailing me since my arrival, but whom I had eluded, having no desire for publicity. It appeared that my trip into the interior was regarded as a great adventure. I couldn't see it that way myself, for as you will realize nothing terribly exciting had occurred. I got out of Bulawayo next morning, and did not see the column and a half of newsprint which detailed my experiences.

I again travelled on the construction train, and on the journey I fell in with a Dutchman, who treated me like a brother. He insisted that I shared his food and his drink. From a canvas bag he produced a large leg of boiled mutton, which he carved with his jack-knife, handing me portions with his fingers. I will say, however, that that mutton was good.

From where the construction train set me down a forty-mile walk lay between me and the Old Drift. I engaged a single carrier to bear my blankets, and after I had covered about twenty miles I had a bad attack of fever which laid me out completely. Fortunately, I was near a river, and could have all the drink I needed. I laid me down in a wretched state, and on the second day my carrier vanished. In those days native boys would not stay by a sick man, but would leave him to his fate.

Alone I lay on the veldt, and at times I think I lapsed into delirium. I had nothing but water to drink, and I couldn't have eaten food even if I had had the energy to prepare any. Four days later my boy reappeared. He had not, as I had assumed, deserted me, but had gone back to Wankie, a two days' trek, to find a doctor and tell him that a white man was dying out on the veldt. The boy's effort was something nobler than the doctor's, for the latter only gave him a note. " Please tell bearer what medicines you want," it ran—surely the last word in futility.

For eight days I lay there, burning with fever, able to move only by the most painful effort, and taking nothing but water. On the ninth day, in the very early morning, a white man came upon me. He was, however, in a great hurry to catch a construction train going south, and after doing what he could he had to leave me. He told me that about a mile away a number of white men were

198

doing preparatory work on a new railway, and I resolved to make the effort to reach their camp.

At six-thirty I started out. I was so weak that I could progress no more than a yard or two at a time. The smallest pebble was big enough to trip me, or I would simply crumple up anyhow. When I fell, it took me a long time to gather strength for rising again. But I stuck it and at four o'clock in the afternoon I reached the camp, though for the last hundred yards or so I was carried in by natives attached to the party who had come upon me at that distance from the camp. It had taken me seven and a half hours to travel something less than a mile. I stopped at the camp for some days, during which I took forty grains of quinine a day. From the effects of the drug I could hardly hear a word that was said to me, and my head felt like a balloon.

This was my worst dose of fever in all my experience of it. When I got back ultimately to the Old Drift my friends scarcely could recognize me. The only being who knew me at once was Flossie.

Flossie was expecting to become a mother. One afternoon she came and sat in front of me with a very pained look in her eyes, and told me all about it. I took her into my hut and fixed her up a comfortable bed in a box, into which she hopped at once. Having seen her thus settled, I left the hut. But it seemed that she hated being without her friend at this juncture, for she came after me like a flash. I went back, saw her settled again, and after a time went away. Again she came after me. It was plain that she expected her master to stand by, and I remained with her until the first pup was born. " Now," I said to myself, " she'll be all right." And I attempted to leave the hut once more. But no. She wasn't letting me go, and I had to turn back with her. I had to remain in the hut until she had delivered the complete litter. The wonderful ' pal-ship ' of dogs is to me an everlasting delight. In a hundred such ways did Flossie tell me that the only thing in the world that mattered to her was myself—her friend and master.

Christmastide, now upon us again, was always a great time at the Old Drift. Sports were held, and every one turned out for the occasion. There were horse races, and races of man against horse, the man running and the horse trotting. Tilting the bucket was an event that everybody liked. The tilter rode in a wheel-barrow and was provided with an assegai which he had to get through a hole in a board under a bucket of water. If he missed the hole and hit the board, of course, the bucket swung round and he was drenched. Then we had donkey races. There were about a dozen donkeys in the camp, but no competitor was allowed to ride his own beast. No reins were allowed and the donks had to be ridden barebacked. I was a competitor. Half-way down the course my donkey, from going well, suddenly baulked. I went clean over the donkey's head, but landed on my feet. I remounted and finished the race, only to be disqualified for leaving my mount.

This was the last Christmas in the old phase of the Old Drift. The railway was approaching, and with it would come a lot of new settlers. I myself was soon to shift my habitation for good to the other side of the river, and take up my quarters by the bridge, Flossie with me. Already people were coming in to wait for the throwing open of North-western Rhodesia to settlers. It was a time of fine opportunity. Pioneers were allowed to select land where they liked in North-western Rhodesia. They were granted 6000 acres at 3*d*. per acre, and were given five years in which to pay. I got, myself, a permit for 6000 acres at this price, but there was a stipulation in the deed of sale whereby one had to occupy the land, and I was not ready to settle down on any one spot. One of the Old Drift campers took the chance and kept on buying land at any price up to 1*s*. an acre. To-day he owns a ranch of anything up to 100,000 acres. Another friend, who selected 6000 acres on the Kafue river, sold his property for £6000 three years later.

After the railway had gone north I got a permit for 2000 acres at a price of 8*d*. per acre five miles away from the line or 1*s*. per acre within that distance, but did not take it up. About a year ago I took the permit to the Lands Department Office for Northern Rhodesia and, as a joke, claimed this land. There was nothing doing! A sort of statute of limitations ruled me out.

CHAPTER XV

THE RAILWAY COMES

IN May of 1904 the final stretch of line to the Victoria Falls was completed, and all the 'Old Drifters' went over to see the last of the sleepers laid and the line linked up. The party that I was with went part of the way by river. As we were passing Long Island we disturbed a hippo which was feeding on it, whereupon the beast plunged into the river and came right under the stern of our boat. That, fortunately, was a beamy old tub and it did not capsize, but myself and my companions were chucked into the air, to land face downward among the floorboards. An upset would have been a costly business for me in more ways than one, for I had three cameras with me.

The completion of the line was a great affair. The engine which followed the plate-layers, highly decorated with palms and flowers, was driven by Miss Pauling, sister of one of the contractors. Its front bore the legend: " We've got a long way to go! "—a reference, of course, to the fact that the section completed was only a part of the Cape-to-Cairo line. As soon as the last sleeper was laid there was celebration, with native sports, mock battles with assegais and knobkerries, then a feast for the whites.

I took a lot of photographs, and did a roaring trade in prints at five shillings a time. The contractors, engineers, and engine-drivers bought copies by the score.

THE BRIDGE COMPLETED

Among the contractors was one 'Bill,' who laid the last sleeper on the Bulawayo-Falls section of the line. Bill, a very good-hearted chap and notably generous, gave me orders for prints to the extent of nineteen pounds, but did not pay for them at the time. A year later, at the first regatta on the Zambesi, I encountered Bill's brother Jack. Jack would have it that I was trying to rob Bill, who, he said, had paid for the photographs. I told Jack that he was in error, and he got annoyed about it. He got so annoyed, in fact, that he went for me bald-headed. I was no match for Jack, but I kept the scrap going as long as I was able. The result was that in lieu of my nineteen pounds I got the biggest hiding I've ever had in my life. Bill, alas! is long since dead, his bill still unpaid.

I had the first meal that was served to a customer at the Victoria Falls hotel. I ate it, I remember, in an annexe to the coal-hole near the kitchen. It was lunch I had, and I paid about four shillings for it.

At the rail-head by the Falls a Customs House was established. I acted as clearing and forwarding agent for Mopani Clarke, of the Old Drift. Mopani's wagon came in under the charge of a young Dutchman, and all I had to do was to clear and check goods out of bond, weighing them, and watch the Dutchman load them into the wagon. For this service I was paid at the rate of one shilling per 100 lb. weight. It was very easy money, which came to a substantial amount each month. The Dutchy had the thick end of the log. One day he was telling me his troubles. " Mr Clark," says he, " do you know I only get five pounds a month and I eat myself ? " I have often wondered how he performed the operation.

The hotel, at the beginning, was simply a long structure of wood and iron containing a dining-room and bar, bedrooms and offices. Later on it was enlarged by the addition of two large engine-sheds removed from railway headquarters. One of these was converted into a dining-room and the other into bedrooms. Later still two annexes of wood and iron were put up, complete with bathrooms, for the *haut ton*. In the hot weather the rooms were ovens, and in the cold, refrigerators—but nobody grumbled much. After all, what could one expect in the heart of Africa? While the bridge was still in course of construction an outside bar was put up for the workmen. They were a rough lot, even for the wilds, and they made the hotel very uncomfortable for sedater guests in the main building, especially just after they got their monthly pay.

At this time the hotel was run by private management. The lessee was an Italian, and the antics of his customers, both heads and hands, kept him scared almost out of his wits. He came into the dining-room on one occasion when the top men on the bridge construction— surveyors, engineers, and the like—were having a social evening. The ' Wop ' was immediately collared by the hilarious assembly, stuck up on the mantelpiece, and commanded to sing a song. Whenever he came in sight of the workmen using the outside bar he was at once chased round the premises. If caught he was hauled into the bar and made to stand drinks all round. He did not relish this rough handling and had not the knack of taking it easily. He therefore gave the outside bar a wide berth, though he must have made a pile from it.

For two or three days after the men received their pay

the bar would be packed. Drinking and gambling went on continuously, with free entertainment day and night for anyone who cared for that sort of thing. There was always a fight going on outside the bar—and the workmen certainly could scrap. Fortunately for the management it had secured the services of an ex-prize fighter as barman. He was not a very big chap, but he stood no nonsense from the crowd. 'Fred' once acted as referee for a fight in which I found myself.

I had missed a very fine little wire-haired terrier pup, and went over to the hotel to see if I could find him. Close to the bar I ran into a workman who was just leaving it. There was a suspicious-looking bulge of something under his coat, and indications that the thing hidden was hairy and white. So I challenged the man with trying to get away with my pup, which proved to be the case, and as he refused to part with it we came to blows. The noise of the battle's opening brought Fred out. I told him to take charge of the pup, which he did. I then had time to attend to my opponent, who was hell bent on giving me what Paddy gave the drum. It was a regular 'up-and-downer' between us, but I was quite sure I was giving more than I was taking. Fred, however, seemed to be of another opinion. "Hit him, P.M.!" he kept saying. "Why don't you hit him! Gaw! Call that a punch!" Thus sarcastically egged on I laid into my man. He took the count, finally, and I got back my pup.

During the building of the bridge Sir Charles Metcalfe stayed at the Falls hotel and he commissioned me to photograph the structure at varying stages of its erection. He often came to my place, and if there were any visitors he was sure to bring them over. He rolled up one day with two of the Coats brothers, the cotton-spinning millionaires, and introduced them with: " Here you are, Clark—two gentlemen with plenty of money. See what you can get out of them." He then went off laughing. Sir Charles was very popular with the men, who called him ' Uncle Charlie,' and he was a very good friend to me.

With the completion of the railway a contingent of the British South African Police was posted for duty. They made camp in huts of the pole and *dagga* type. Their advance guard, so to speak, was a chap called ' Tubby,' who arrived weeks ahead of the others. A great boy was Tubby, and he and I soon became good friends. He would come over to my place and parade up and down with me outside it as if doing sentry-go, talking all the time. His talk very largely was of what he meant to do when he got home. Poor Tubby, he was only a youngster. One night he sent for me to go over and see him. I found him in bed with a fever which he maintained was of the blackwater sort. To cheer him up I pooh-poohed the idea, did what I could for him, and left him a good deal brighter. Next day I had to go away on a journey, and in my absence some friends took Tubby to Livingstone hospital, where he died before night.

If I had been on the spot I should never have permitted him to be moved. I'd had a lot of experience of blackwater fever, and it was my opinion—which I still retain—that anyone down with it should not be moved. Case after case I have seen of sufferers being shifted to hospital or to some settlement, who invariably died. In the conditions then prevailing, when blackwater was suspected the only course was to leave the patient alone. This was especially important where the patient happened to be out on the veldt or away from camp. It was invariably fatal to do more than make him as comfortable as one could—*where he was.* One might keep on giving him hot water, and loads of it—nothing else usually being available—but where a doctor was within reach it was the height of folly to take the patient to the medico. The dodge was to bring the medico to the patient. Of course, with the smoothness of modern ambulance transport, and with the up-to-date therapy, all that may be altered. But of this I am certain. It was, and I imagine it still is, fatal to move a blackwater case in anything like pioneering conditions. I have no shadow of doubt that poor old Tubby was killed by the kind intentions of his ignorant friends.

The police contingent which came after Tubby was seven in number. Keeping order at the Falls did not exercise them much. Once they had to arrest a man who was working on the bridge. They had only a pole and *dagga* hut to put him in, so they leg-ironed him for the night. In the darkness he escaped, leg-irons and all. Next day the detachment under the corporal hunted for him all over the countryside, but without success. In the early hours of the morning that followed the corporal looked out of his window. On the fence six feet away from him dangled the leg-irons. Whether the offender was too honest a man to take away Government property or merely gifted with an acute sense of humour I cannot guess, but he was never caught.

Among amusing memories of the police contingent is

an incident connected with the building of one of my
huts. The operations were being supervised by a trooper,
who acted as my clerk of the works in his spare time.
One day, in company with this trooper, I was coming
away from one of my frequent visits to the police camp
when I spotted, outside the corporal's hut, a very nice
window-frame. It was just what I wanted for the new
building, and my clerk of the works agreed with me. In
due course the hut was finished and the corporal was
asked over to inspect it and have a ' sundowner.' While
putting back his drink he suddenly spotted the window.
It was draped with curtains, but he recognized it.

"Well, I'm damned!" said he. "So it was you, was
it, you blighter, that pinched my window!"

"How the devil did you recognize it" I asked.

"How the devil shouldn't I recognize it?" he replied.
"I had a hell of a job pinching it myself in the first
place!"

The window had come from a dismantled hut belong-
ing to the Cleveland Bridge Company.

The magistrate at Kalomo, a hundred miles or so
north of the Old Drift, had a native to deport. As he
was going home on leave he brought the man down with
him, and saw to it that he crossed the river into Southern
Rhodesia. On his way through the magistrate, who was
on friendly terms with me, warned me about this native
boy, saying that he was the biggest rogue in Northern
Rhodesia, an expert thief and burglar. I made it my
business to go over to police headquarters and pass the
warning on to the corporal. He sent the word round the
camp and told his men to be on the *qui vive*.

That same evening I had some friends in for a game of poker. When they went and I retired to my sleeping-tent I found that the deportee had been through all my clothes and belongings. It was his wily habit, however, never to 'lift' anything but money, and all mine, of course, had been with me at the poker table. So I lost nothing—at least, through the nigger. His operations on the hotel, however, were more successful. Each new batch of guests—unless they securely locked their doors at night—had their rooms gone through by a thief, presumably the native burglar. Good hauls were made, as much as twenty to thirty pounds at a time. Of course, the native, being a known criminal, was taken hold of and searched. No money, however, was found on him at any time.

The police corporal determined to get the man red-handed, as it were, and for several nights he lay under the hotel, which stood on three-foot piles, with his face blackened. At long last his patience was rewarded; he saw the boy get into the hotel and waited for him to come out. He then gave him a knock with his army revolver and grabbed him by the pants. Two native police, who were also lying in wait, now rushed up and together they secured the burglar. But though he subsequently got a long sentence, the stolen money was never recovered.

There is an odd story about the magistrate who brought this native down for deportation. He wanted the head of an eland to complete his collection. Now the eland is royal game, and having stalked and shot a specimen my friend had committed an offence. He was the only magistrate in a very large district, and the

O

offence was within his jurisdiction. His duty, as he conceived it, lay clear before him. He reported himself to the police, tried and found himself guilty—and imposed on himself a fine of ten pounds, or one month's imprisonment. He paid the fine, and hung up the eland's head.

The first through train from Cape Town arrived with a large party. The journey was apparently a great adventure for these good people; the train was placarded through all its length and on both sides with legends informing the world how wonderful it was.

On the Sunday I was visited by many of the excursionists, who bought photographs of the Falls. One gentleman betrayed great interest in an album of views which I had made up. He asked me its price. I told him my charge was five pounds.

" I never trade on Sundays," said this pious gentleman. " It is against my principles."

" What a pity! " I replied. " It is the last album I have, and it is sure to be snapped up. But I have plenty of loose photographs that you can buy to-morrow."

" If it wasn't Sunday," said he, " I would give you four pounds for it."

" Since it is Sunday, however," I said, " you ought to pay more—to salve your conscience. My price is five pounds."

He hung round for some time with his ' ifs ' and ' peradventures,' but I gave him no encouragement.

" Well," he sighed at last, " I suppose I'll have to pay your price."

And pay it he did. I have often envied him his conscience—at least, as regards its flexibility.

THE MAIN FALL

The first great lady of the many I have met at the Falls was Princess Christian. She came by special train in 1904, and I was commanded to bring post cards and photographs to the royal train for her inspection. In those rough-and-ready days few of us had complete suits to our names, and I was in like case with the majority. I was in a quandary. I couldn't very well appear before her Royal Highness in khaki slacks and a shirt, so I hunted round the camp to collect what decent togs I could borrow or steal. From a police trooper I borrowed a jacket, got a collar and tie from some one else, and an item of clothing here and there until at last I had the complete outfit in which to present myself to Royalty. Not Solomon in all his glory could have been arrayed as I was that time!

The interview was satisfactory in its results for both parties to it, but when I told the aide-de-camp afterwards about my search for a rig-out he roared with laughter. He told the Princess the story subsequently, and I heard that it amused her hugely.

In the following year the first regatta was held on the Zambesi. Crews came from all parts of Africa to compete, and there were close on a thousand visitors altogether. The capacity of the hotel was good only for about a hundred of these, so the rest had to camp out. By the second day the hotel was cleaned of beer and whisky, and food had almost run out. I was invited by a friend to dine there. The feast was worthy of the rude fellow's grace: "Gawd! What a meal!" I wished I had invited my friend to my own place. The service was terrible, with a wait of twenty minutes between each of the courses. These were: soup—with the taste and appearance of weak Bovril; one bony cutlet and half a potato; biscuits and cheese with no butter. There wasn't a scrap of butter in the hotel, no joints, no poultry. For this magnificent (!) spread we were charged seven-and-six apiece. I'd sooner have bought a marriage licence.

Along the regatta course were the usual ' joints '— poker tables, ' Under and Over,' ' Crown and Anchor,' canteens, and the side-shows. The concessionaires, so to call them, must have raked in pots of money.

I was besieged in my huts by Bulawayo friends who could not get accommodation in the hotel. They dossed down in rows and tiers in my huts, and all about them, and in the kitchen. Several had brought along their own nosebags, and foodstuffs in bottle were plentiful, but my larder was sadly depleted. I had to feed them ultimately on bully beef and hard tack. But, as the saying is: " A good time was enjoyed by all! "

The formal opening of the bridge coincided with the visit of the British Association to Africa for their Conference, and Professor Darwin was asked to declare the bridge open. With him, to witness the ceremony, came most of the Asses—as the members of the Association are called—and among them I met several old friends. I had to introduce myself to them, for they would never have recognized me. Since leaving Bulawayo for the Falls and Barotseland I had grown a beard—a face fungus that was beautiful in patches only. I looked like a back-veldt Boer, besides being emaciated by fever. From averaging ten stone, normally, I was down to just over seven.

I had arranged to leave for England and Home

immediately after the function, and the night before my departure I was lying in my hut getting over still another bout of fever. About nine o'clock one of my pals came in.

" Come on, P.M., over to my camp," he said. " There's a fellow just turned up looking for a game of poker. There's only the three of us, and we must have a fourth."

" Leave me out, old man," I said. " I feel too darned bad—really I do."

" Ah, come along, P.M.! " says he. " It'll be your last chance for a game before you leave."

I begged to be left alone in peace and quiet, but my friend was insistent. It was not heartlessness on his part, but only that fever was so common with us—it was about a weekly thing with most of us—that we thought nothing of it. Very likely if it had been this pal who was down and myself that wanted the game of poker I'd have acted just as he did. In any case, he kept at me, and at last I gave way.

" All right," I said, " I'll come. But, win or lose, I won't play for a second after midnight."

" Righto! " said he.

I didn't trouble even to dress, but simply got into an overcoat and went over with my pal to his hang-out.

At twelve o'clock, eighty pounds to the good, I got up to go home. The others protested, but I was adamant. I really was ill and longing to get back to bed. They saw me home and into bed. Next morning they took me to the train—and I thanked them warmly for paying my fare home.

CHAPTER XVI

HOME FOR A WIFE

IT may be imagined with what happiness I found myself on the boat bound for England and Home. There was, to begin with, the fact that I was going home for a wife—a girl to whom I had been engaged for four years. I had pressed her to come out to Africa for the wedding, but she had insisted that if I wanted her I would have to fetch her. Then, again, Africa had taken sad toll of my health. I was so done that it looked as if I was liable to peg out on small cause.

I was still a fairly disreputable wisp of humanity when I boarded that boat. I had made up my mind to defer buying clothes until I reached England, so there I was—in reach-me-downs hanging on my skeleton, and with that beard. As touching the latter, I had been warned by the home contingent that if I turned up with it I wouldn't be received, but I was determined to take it to England with me. I had not told the folks I was coming home. The first intimation they would get would be from Southampton.

On the boat, in the usual way, I made some very good friends. I had brought with me from Rhodesia a good supply of biltong—strips of buck-meat, sun-dried—and at nights when the ship's bars and kitchen offices were closed down our select group used to meet together in my cabin. We would sit up to all hours, chewing biltong, and well-nigh yarning our heads off.

One day at afternoon tea in the saloon, Teneriffe being abeam, I found myself in ' the shakes '—the ague which ushers in an attack of malaria. I turned to a man nicknamed ' Scroggs,' who was my particular pal. " Come on, Scroggs—lend me a hand—I've got malaria coming on." Scroggs got me to my cabin and into bed. We rang for the cabin-steward. When he came I issued orders: six blankets, a dozen Schweppes, six pegs of champagne, and a big chunk of ice. These were to keep the sweat going once it started on me. But the sweat this time refused to break out. I dosed myself with aspirin and about stifled myself with a covering of blankets; but not one bead of moisture would break out on my wretched body. It was three o'clock in the morning, eleven hours after I got to bed, that the blessed relief came.

I need hardly say what a rotten experience fever is, with pains all over one, a thick head, and a general sense of wretchedness. But once the sweat came I kept it going with the Schweppes and bubbly.

About four o'clock the following afternoon I felt better. but still deplorably weak. I was sitting on the edge of my bunk, my legs dangling over the side, trying to make up my mind whether to get up or not. I hated the notion of lying in bed, but I still was seedy. I simply couldn't summon the will to make a decision either way. Suddenly the ship's doctor came bustling in.

" What's the matter here? " he demanded. " I heard some one was dying."

" Nobody's dying that I know of," said I, " and nothing much is the matter, Doc. I have had a touch of fever, that's all."

215

"Why didn't you send for me? I know all about fever."

"I reckon I do, too," said I.

"And I reckon I know a damned sight more than you do!"

With that he stamped out of the cabin. He didn't speak to me again for the rest of the voyage.

We were due to arrive at Southampton in the early morning. I didn't go to bed at all the previous night. I simply couldn't. I was too excited. I stood on deck the night through, watching for the first sight of land. I saw the lights of the Channel spring up, and the pilot come aboard. It all brought a lump into my throat— Home again after five years in the wilds! No stay-at-home can know what the experience means.

We berthed at dawn. Farewells were exchanged with fellow passengers, and arrangements made for future meetings. In the train the folk in my compartment fell to discussing their plans, but I could not speak. All I wanted to do was to take my fill of England. After the far horizons of Rhodesia, and the wide spaces, the English countryside seemed to be cast in miniature. The fields, with their hedges round them and the haystacks in their corners looking like native huts, were about the size of pocket-handkerchiefs. I kept saying to myself: "This is Home—this is Home!"

Upon arrival at Southampton I had wired to a brother in London. This was the first intimation to members of the family that I was to be expected. When the boat-train drew in my brother was on the platform to welcome me, beard and all, and he saw me into the train for Cambridge. Unheralded in any way, I simply opened the door of the ancestral home—and walked in. I need not elaborate on the surprise I gave the family that Saturday afternoon.

My next move, of course, was to the home of my *fiancée*, and here again I need not elaborate the details of our meeting. I had known my future wife for ump-teen years, and I had no reason to feel dissatisfied with the welcome she gave me. But she wasn't having any of my beard and I had immediate orders to go and have it removed. More necessary from my point of view was new clothes.

The reception I got at the outfitters as a result of turning up in my 'slops' amused me mightily. I don't think the assistants were to be blamed for taking me to be worth less than twopence-ha'penny—I must have looked it! I wanted some boiled shirts. "These are three shillings and sixpence." "What about something better?" I asked. "These are four shillings and six-pence." And so they went up by degrees timorously. "Give me the best!" I said. It was some time ere it dawned on the assistants that I really wanted to turn out in style, and the same hesitation about producing the superior articles was noticeable in all departments. But by the time I was reaching the end of the round in the store the best was being produced first. The rumour had spread that the tough had money to burn.

In a rash moment before leaving England five years previously I had promised a friend, President of a society in Cambridge, that if I ever returned I would lecture to the members. I was now reminded of the promise, and my friend threw a thorough scare into me.

I begged to be let off; I had nothing to lecture about; I had never lectured; I never wanted to lecture. My protestations were futile. I was held to my promise and a date was fixed for the event.

For the fortnight before the lecture I spent hours daily trying to write up my theme. But I couldn't get a word on paper, and even headings eluded me. I groaned and sweated over the thing, fruitlessly, until I was in despair. By good chance, however, I had made some lantern slides. There was nothing else for it but to show the pictures and vamp the rest.

The dreaded evening came round. To be certain of my turning up, my friend the President came to fetch me. He found me dithering with fright, and agreed that heroic measures might be necessary. These were taken at a pub., where I put back a couple of stiff whiskies and soda. I also insisted that there should be another stiff one on the table from which I was to deliver the talk. I needed all the courage, Dutch or otherwise, that I could muster.

There was nothing in the scene at the lecture hall to deliver me from my state of funk. The place was packed. People were sitting in the aisle, the gallery was overflowing, and people had been turned away from the doors. My own folks and the bulk of my friends were in the front rows, and there were some of the Cambridge members of the British Association there too. To lecture to strangers would have been bad enough—but to my own kindred and friends! . . .

I was introduced to the audience by the President, the lights were turned down, and I began. For the first five minutes I was so shaky that my friend, as he confessed later, expected me to break down at any moment. Somehow or other, luckily, I did at last get going, and began to feel that the audience was interested. Then, all at once, I was through. " Good garden stuff ! " I said to myself. " I have hardly filled in twenty minutes ! " The lights went up and, glancing at the clock on the gallery front, I discovered I had been at it for an hour and forty —and the whisky on the table stood untouched. When the President got up, however, to thank me my nervousness came back in full flood. I had been well acquainted with the hall in the old days and I decided to escape round the back of the screen. I remembered a door by which the orchestra got on the platform from the basement, and I made for that. But during my absence in Africa this door had been built up, and, crestfallen, I had to return ignominiously to the front of the screen.

An old school friend happened to be in the audience, and after the lecture he sought me out. He was, he said, a director of the Sunday Lecture League, and he thought my stuff was good enough for his Association. The lectures under its ægis were given in the Alhambra Theatre, Leicester Square, London. If I liked, said this old friend, he would fix a date for me. I was not very sanguine about his ability to pull this off, but he did. I considered the engagement a great honour. My appointed Sunday fell between one on which Darwin was the lecturer and another when Harry Furniss of *Punch* fame did his stuff.

By the time the great day arrived I had gained a lot of experience, having travelled to various parts of England to talk of my African adventures. It was lucky for me that I had become hardened to audiences, because the front seats at my Alhambra lecture were filled almost exclusively by Rhodesians home on leave. They all knew me, more or less, and they were there with every intention of ragging me. As I went on with the lecture remarks floated up to the platform: " Come off it! " " Ooh! You damned liar! " " Ought to know better at your time o' life! " " Oi! What about a quick one, P.M.? "

They kept it going all through, and without my experience with country audiences it would have embarrassed me a lot. As it was, the interjections amused rather than worried me, and put me in fine fettle. I replied *sotto voce* when I could with: " Meet me afterwards, boys! " and so on.

The lecture was a definite success. After it was over I left the theatre by the stage entrance to seek the gang. They left by the front to seek for me. But we must have played ' round the mulberry bush ' about the block, because we missed each other.

One of the most interesting of my lecture dates was at the Mission to Seamen's Institute, Poplar, close to the docks in the East India Road. I had gone to visit an old Cambridge friend who was honorary chaplain to the Institute, and it was he who asked me to give my lecture there. The hall was crowded with seamen of all nationalities and hues, even to three or four niggers as black as the ace of spades. But the reception was enthusiastic, and the lecture went with a bang. It was a delight to watch the faces of that hard-boiled crowd.

After my show my parson friend and myself were mixing with the crowd, chatting to them, when up rolls an old salt to accost the chaplain.

" Well, young man," says he, " it's a nice easy job you've got—no work and plenty of pay ! "

" I'd change jobs with you readily," said my friend. " I don't get paid for this. I do it because I like it, and for the chance it gives me to meet fellows like yourself. "

" Well, then," the old shell-back replied, " your dad should've put you to something better ! "

I was going up to Town by train one Monday to interview a director of the British South African Company at London Wall. I got into the dining-car smoking section and sat by myself, reading a daily paper. Two men came in, obviously farmers, and seated themselves at the far end of the compartment. I took it that they were headed for the corn market held each Monday at Mark Lane. Then an old parson came in and found a seat close to them. I began to feel my isolation, so I got up and went over to them. I said I was a bit lonely, and asked if they would mind me joining them. They were quite cordial and told me to sit down. I did so, but went on reading my paper.

Presently the conversation took the curious turn of speculation on how long it took to sail from Southampton to Cape Town. The guesses made were of the wildest, so I put down my paper and butted in.

" Gentlemen," I said, " I can answer the question exactly. It takes seventeen days by mail-boat, twenty-one by intermediate steamer."

" Do you know Cape Town ? " one of the farmers asked at once.

" No, I can't say I do—but I came through it quite recently."

" Do you know the Victoria Falls ? " the next question

came like a shot. That was rather a long jump, surely—Cape Town to the Falls being 1600 miles.

" Yes, I ought to," I replied. " I live there."

" Do you know a fellow there named Clark? "

That was another startler, but I answered quite quietly.

" I ought to know him," I said. " That's me ! "

" Oh, I don't mean you," said the farmer, " but another fellow—Fred Clarke."

" I ought to know him, too, for I've lived with him for six months on end. Only—our name for him is Mopani Clarke."

" Well," said the farmer, " he's my brother-in-law."

That same day I was lunching with the general manager of W. H. Smith and Son. I called for him about five minutes before the appointed time, and his secretary came out to tell me he was engaged for a few minutes. The secretary looked at me for a moment or two.

" You come from Rhodesia, don't you? " he asked.

" I do," said I.

" I wonder," said he, " if you know a great friend of mine there? "

" Well," I grinned, " Rhodesia's rather a large country, you know—close on a million square miles. Eight hundred and eighty thousand square miles, to be exact."

" Man I mean is called Kerry—Frank Kerry."

And there it was—the second odd coincidence that day. Frank Kerry had stayed with me for six months, and I had nursed him for a fortnight before I could get a doctor to him when he had typhoid fever.

I might well recount here another of my odd experiences at home. I was for a few days with my brother who lived just outside London. One night we were going home from a theatre in our glad rags. Just before we reached the house we came to a very nice-looking hotel. I suggested a night-cap, and my brother fell in with the notion, so we went into the saloon bar, where a few customers were lined up. My brother wanted a beer and I wanted a whisky and soda. I passed the order to the man behind the bar counter—he was, as I afterwards discovered, the hotel proprietor. Instead of measuring me out a tot in the usual way from the inverted bottles on the ledge of the shelf, he planked a whisky bottle and glass down in front of me.

" What's this? " said I. " I thought you measured spirits—— "

" Not to you, sir," said he.

" What the deuce do you mean? "

" Not to a Rhodesian, sir—— "

" What on earth are you talking about? " I said, and he smiled.

" No good, sir," he replied. " You're from Rhodesia, sir, I'll bet. I can always spot a Rhodesian."

" You're right, of course," I admitted, " but it's a licker to me. How did you know? "

" I have been in Rhodesia. I was in the B.S.A. Police for three years."

" Join up! " said I, helping myself and shoving the bottle to him. We had a real old chin-wag.

The bottle was always handed to the customer in the old days of Rhodesia. But how that chap picked me out in my evening clothes as a Rhodesian I cannot make out to this day.

I remember getting ' the shakes ' one evening in Town.
I was in Newgate Street when they came on, and I
turned into a chemist's shop and asked for a clinical
thermometer. Having bought one, I took my temperature there and then. It showed 103 degrees. I asked the
chemist for fifteen grains of quinine.

" Fifteen grains—what for? " he asked, pop-eyed.

" To take," I said. " I have a dose of fever, temperature 103. Let me have fifteen grains of quinine,
please, and a glass of water."

" But fifteen grains will kill you! " he said.

" Nonsense! " I replied. " I've taken forty grains
daily for eight days on end."

Very reluctantly he supplied me with the fifteen
grains, but said I ought to go to hospital.

" Hospital nothing! " said I. " I can look after myself.
I'll go home."

" How far have you to go? " he asked.

" Only about fifty miles," I said.

The chemist nearly dropped. But I got home all right
and went to bed so quietly that my people did not know
I was there until next morning.

I was married on February 15, 1906, at Great Saint
Andrew's church, Cambridge, to Kate French, daughter
of Henry French, Solicitor and Clerk of the Peace
in that city. I was at the church on time, but, as
is usually the case, the bride was a few minutes late.
Standing for that time in full view of the congregation
I felt an awful fool. The bride arrived, and the knot was
tied. But I was in such a dither that, as I have been told,
I did not even offer my bride my arm as we were leaving

the vestry. I always had 'country' manners. Our honeymoon was spent in Devonshire at Teignmouth in the ' House nearest the sea,' and we had a glorious time. A month later we sailed for Africa.

When I came away from the Falls I had left my place in charge of a young Colonial recommended to me by my old Geelong pal, Arthur Weiner, who came from the same town as myself, and whom and his family I had known practically all my life. Weiner told me that this friend of his was as straight as a gun-barrel, a recommendation which was good enough for me.

I had been making good money at the Falls, for the railway was bringing a constant stream of visitors from all over the world. But month after month went by of my leave and no cash reached me from the Falls. I wrote and cabled, but all I got was a few lame letters. After eight months, by the time I was to leave England with my bride, I was broke. I was so broke, in fact, that I had to borrow thirty pounds from a maiden aunt to see my wife and myself comfortably through.

We arrived at Victoria Falls in April only to find that my "straight as a gun-barrel" manager had bolted a fortnight previously. He had sold all my furniture and exhausted nearly all my stock. He had stolen my shotgun and taken even my dog. I traced him a long way. He had crossed the river, ' borrowing ' a wagon and a span of oxen, and had disappeared into the country up North. At long last I found he was at Mongu in Barotseland, where he had obtained a Government appointment. I wrote there and outlined the situation, but as soon as the rumour reached him that things were stirring he bolted once again. I never caught him. It would have afforded me small material satisfaction, anyway, to have laid him by the heels; it would merely have put me to additional expense.

But at the moment of our arrival there it was. There it undoubtedly was. I had brought my young wife to an empty home, a bare shell without even a bed, and no more furniture than a few poor pieces made from packing cases. We had no money, and the business I had created was practically a ruin. A fine situation, surely, for a young wife to have to face!

CHAPTER XVII

MY WIFE AND I

A MARRIED man, I've often noticed, is as good a man as his wife will make him. I knew I had married a girl of quality, but those days of facing the dire situation created by that decamping manager were quickly to prove what fine qualities my wife possessed.

I suggested going to the hotel until our huts could be refurnished from Bulawayo. I knew my credit was good with the hotel, and that in the circumstances I would be trusted up to a substantial amount. But my wife would have none of the hotel. My hutment was her home, and she would make the best of it. So we took over possession, *sans* bed, *sans* money—*sans* pretty well anything but hope and a fine spirit of comradeship.

About the only stock we had in hand was a considerable number of post cards. Within a week, to augment this, I got together a fair collection of native curios. Then my wife had a brain-wave. She suggested selling mahogany beans in the pod. These beans are black with a red cap, and they are very pretty indeed in the pod, which is a broad one, holding from six to a dozen beans. The red cap, attaching each bean to the pod, covers about a third of the bean's length. Together we collected a couple of sacks of these pods from the veldt.

An excursion from the Cape was due to arrive late

one evening and, the hotel being full, most of the passengers had to sleep in the train. I had the station bookstall, and I opened it that night with my wife and myself behind the counter. We did a roaring trade in pictorial post cards at four shillings a dozen and mahogany beans at threepence per pod. That first night we took twenty-eight pounds, and as the excursionists stopped three or four nights at the Falls our takings altogether served to put us on a fair footing. As time went on we got our huts comfortably furnished and became thoroughly settled, but I have never forgotten—nor will I ever forget —the spirit with which my wife, fresh from a very comfortable home in England, faced those first days of discomfort, trial, and uncertainty.

It must not be thought, however, that with the business beginning to build up again my wife's trials were over. I was still full of fever and frequently went down with it. It often happened when in fever that I would become delirious, and the first time my wife found me babbling she became thoroughly alarmed. She was so scared that she sent a runner off to Livingstone, nine miles away, for a doctor. The doctor was a friend of mine; clever as they make them; he was P.M.O. for North-western Rhodesia, and a great figure in the province. He was an Irishman, as anyone could immediately tell, with a great command of words and a blunt way of using them. His habitual garb was a grey jacket and white trousers; he was seldom seen but with his white bags creased concertina fashion, and never without his monocle.

In answer to my wife's summons he duly and promptly arrived, but by that time I was getting back to normal.

" Phwat's the matter with ye, Clark? "

"Nothing," I said. "Only a touch of fever."

"Thin phwat the hell are ye after sendin' for me?"

"I didn't send for you—I didn't want you," I told him.

"Who did, thin?"

"My wife, I suppose. I was a bit delirious, and that scared her perhaps."

He looked me over, all the same.

"You'll do," he said, with his delightful brogue. "Ye know what to do as well as I do, so I'll be off."

A month or so later he was over at the Falls and he dropped into our establishment for a cup of tea. Before he left I proffered him a couple of guineas. This was the usual fee for a doctor to come from Livingstone to the Falls, and by no means an exorbitant one since the visit entailed fully half a day. The doctor rescrewed his monocle in his eye the better to scowl at the offered money.

"What's this for?" he demanded.

"Your fee for coming over to see me when I had fever."

"But ye got my bill, didn't ye?"

"Yes, but I haven't looked at it," said I. "I know very well what the fee is."

"Ye'd better look at my bill now, thin!"

I found the bill and opened it for the first time. It was made out for half a guinea.

"What's the idea, Doc.?" I said. "This is for only half a guinea!"

"Quite right, too," was the doctor's reply. "Ye weren't dam'-well bad enough to be charged two guineas!"

This was our Irish doctor all over. He was a damned good sort to his very core. He had all the Irishman's fine qualities, including that of causing laughter. I remember that he once got into a situation which suggested the start of a nudist club. True the club existed for no more than a minute or two, and had a membership of one. It happened this way: one morning, while the doctor was having his bath, a severe earth tremor shook the buildings of the settlement. The inhabitants popped out of their dwellings like rabbits from a well-ferreted warren. Among them was the doctor—in his birthday suit. I'd have given a lot to have seen that; I'll bet whatever else he wasn't wearing he was not without his monocle.

Livingstone, where the doctor dwelt, became a centre of social activity in the early days. The township was the Old Drift settlement shifted to the sand belt five miles from the original site. The new location was altogether healthier, being higher and drier than the old swampy place. My wife and I went to dances and dinners there, travelling to the northern bank by canoe and on to the township by cart. Social gatherings were of all sorts and frequent at Livingstone, for the pioneers were a jovial lot. There were dances at the court-house, and we often were invited to functions at Government House. On such visits we had to put up at the hotel. This consisted of a few rooms, a bar and a dining-room, all built of poles and *dagga*. All classes were represented in the dining-room, from the one local barrister to the one local bricklayer. The bar was a rowdy place. When, as a married man, one passed it, one could see its counter crowded with men tossing for drinks, its corners occupied with others singing raucously and out of tune, while benches, and even the floor, were laden with those who had ' passed out.'

At The Huts, our residence at the Falls, we often had nightly visitors. Some of them were not very welcome. At this time the bush about the settlement had not been cleared to any extent, and jackals would come and sit, giving tongue to their weird and very exasperating yowling. I would get up, go out, and fire in the direction of the howling, which, for the moment, would cease. But I would be no sooner settled down again than the chorus would rise up as exasperating as ever.

We had a couple of cows that we kraaled just outside our fence. The scent of them often brought lions round in the dark hours. We also had fowls, and leopards came after those—with more success than the lions. At the back of our place, about three hundred yards off, was the police camp, with donkeys and horses used for patrol work. The smell of them was an additional attraction for the lions.

Three young bloods decided one lovely moonlit night to sit up and get the lions that came on the prowl about the police camp practically every night. They climbed—the young bloods, not the lions—to the roof of the stables with a full equipment. This included a bottle of whisky, and the hunters must have fortified themselves well, for they were fast asleep when the lions turned up. Oh, yes! The lions turned up all right, because their spoor was to be seen all around the stables in the morning. Which goes to prove a quite elderly axiom that one cannot mix whisky with lion-hunting.

There was one particular leopard, specializing in fowl-stealing, that I made up my mind to get. This fellow was getting away with about four birds a night, and we also lost two turkeys and a cat. It was no great idea, this of giving rations to a leopard, so one night I determined to sit up for him.

My wife insisted on sharing the vigil. At ten o'clock we took up stations in the hut that stood nearest to the fowls' roosting-place, my wife at one window and myself at another. Half an hour went by, and we heard the squawk of one fowl meeting its doom. Sixty minutes or so more went by, then my wife got an awful scare as she sat by the open window. Something sprang up out of the dark on to her hand as it lay on the window sill. It was only our second cat, however. After that my wife came and sat beside me and we watched together. Another fifteen minutes passed, then my wife whispered that she saw something moving, and pointed it out to me. I peered into the darkness for some time, then declared the object to be the stump of a tree. We continued our vigil, and after a while I noticed that the supposed stump seemed to be moving gradually nearer and nearer to us. As the moments went by the object definitely showed up nearer, and there was no ' seeming ' about it. It was a leopard sure enough. The situation was exceedingly tense, and the nerves of both of us were strung like banjo-strings. That leopard was certainly in no hurry. Nearer and nearer it came until, from the low window, I could have leaned out and touched it with my hand. I had let it get so near, in fact, that when I cautiously raised my gun I could not put it to my shoulder. I hoisted it to an acute angle and touched it off with my thumb. A flash and a bang, and the leopard disappeared. Not that we saw him go. One moment he was there, and the next he wasn't. We got a light and examined the spot he had so hastily vacated, and found what looked like some of his entrails. These we covered with a dish and betook ourselves to bed to wait for morning.

In the morning's light we lifted the dish and found that we had covered the remains of the first fowl which the leopard had taken, and which he had been chewing preparatory to securing and absorbing his second course.

As I have said, our habitations were surrounded at this period by thick bush. I searched in the more immediate portions of the bush, but came on no trace of the leopard. There was a good chance that he had been merely wounded and had got away, but, with the awkward angle at which I held the gun, just as likely a chance perhaps that I had not hit him at all. I had about sixty boys working for me at this time on a special job, and I turned them all out to help in the search. But we failed to trace the brute, and at last I gave up and called in the searchers.

But soon after I got back to the hutment the wife of our house-boy came rushing up to tell my wife that she had seen the leopard lying fast asleep. Gun in hand I went with her to the spot, and approached with due caution. The woman had pointed to a place within about thirty yards of the huts, and sure enough there lay the leopard, a beauty, apparently fast asleep. It was stone dead, and it was not a 'him,' but a 'her'—a fine female leopard, seven feet four inches in length, with a splendidly marked coat. My search with the boys had started

233

well beyond the place where she lay. The thickness of the bush close to the house had made it very easy to miss her.

I shot another leopard from my bedroom window several years later. This was another fowl-stealer who had taken heavy toll of the hen-roost for three nights running. On the fourth night together with a companion I sat up to receive the marauder. Two traps had been set at the gate of the fence, and our guns could cover the whole of the yard. But the prowler seemed to have no desire for close acquaintanceship. He did his prowling well out of sight, though not without intervals for re-freshment.

For three nights my friend and I kept vigil, but without result. We were thoroughly tired by the morning of the fourth day, and we decided to have a rest that night. I myself was nearly dead with want of sleep and got to bed early. At about ten o'clock, when I lay so drugged in slumber that not the Last Trump would have wakened me, the fowl-stealer could be heard doing his round. My wife did what the Last Trump would have failed to do. She woke me. She got me, grumbling, out of bed, and persuaded me to take up my watch again. It says a lot for her persuasive powers, because I felt like nothing on earth—unless it were a piece of chewed string. Time went by, heavy-footed, and nothing happened. Then at 1.40 in the morning the visitor, apparently alive to the presence of traps, cleared the fence, landed on the kitchen roof, and thence to a tree. Here he bagged a fowl, and there was silence for a time. It came to four o'clock, and then the beast could be heard stealing round the yard and about the

LEOPARD SHOT AT THE HUTS

huts. He helped himself to a second ration and disappeared without exposing himself to view.

At 5.40 a.m. a third visit was heralded by the usual squawk; but this time the leopard was seen as he seized the fowl and he got a charge of buckshot in his hindquarters. Surprise must have robbed him of his usual caution, for, instead of clearing the fence in his habitual way when coming or going, he bolted to the fence gate and into a spring trap. Until dawn he could be heard roaring and grumbling with pain and rage as, dragging the trap with him, he explored all corners of the house clearing. The weight of the trap was too heavy to let him move far, but eventually he did succeed in breaking through the reed fence. When there was light enough to permit a sight of him he was dispatched with rifle fire. Then it was discovered that he was a full-grown leopard, very fat and in fine condition. And well he might be. He had been, so to speak, stall fed.

We were expecting a youngster to arrive. Naturally, this was the most wonderful thing that could happen in the world, and of course ours would be the most wonderful child in the world. We were sure it would be a boy, and we decided to call him 'Jimmy.' The great event drew near and all preparations possible were made. But when the time came we had to send seventy miles away for the doctor. It was a beautiful boy, weighing seven and a half pounds, and he had lovely black hair. But he lived only a few minutes. . . . To hear my wife was pitiful. We had tame guinea-fowl in the yard, and she thought their calling was the crying of the baby. We buried 'Jimmy' in the garden of the hotel, there being no consecrated ground. Then some one made remarks that touched us on the raw, and we reburied the baby in our own garden.

A year or two later a second child was expected. My wife had a good deal of fever in those early days, and this resulted in the birth happening prematurely. I had to send hurriedly to Livingstone for the doctor. At the same time I sent a message to the one other woman in the place, but she was down with fever and could not leave her bed. I was mad with anxiety, and the child was born before the doctor reached us. When he did arrive he seemed to me so slow and deliberate that I cursed him up and down. But he knew his job. It was just my anxiety that made him seem so slow. I had to be midwife. That was no job for a young husband. Still, my experience was nothing compared with what my wife went through, for pioneering is especially hard on a woman. This time it was a girl child.

Two nights before our elder son was born there was a terrific storm at the Falls. We were sitting in our thatched hut playing dominoes. I had four matadors, I remember, and it was my ' down.' Suddenly, without the slightest warning, there came a vivid flash of lightning, and right on the heels of it a most appalling crash of thunder. This frightened my wife, and the game was abandoned. Now came the rain, a terrific and continuous torrential downpour, and an accompaniment of thunder and lightning, awful to hear and behold. The rain was more like a waterspout than even tropical rain. Within five hours no less than seven and a half inches had fallen, which is twenty-five per cent. of the average rainfall which we get in a season of five months. So bad was the downpour that the hotel, which stands back from the gorge about a hundred yards, had a deep gully from twenty-five to thirty feet deep, and about as wide, washed away on either side of it. Had the rain lasted much longer the cuttings must have reached the hotel itself, possibly with disastrous results. In all my African years, or indeed in all my life, I have never seen such a a dreadful storm—and I hope never to see a tempest like it again. The rain pounded through the thatch of our roof as if it had been merely a net. My wife and I decided to get to bed. Our nearest exit from the thatched hut to the sleeping one was through the window, and we negotiated that. Attempting to keep dry was useless, and we stepped out into water that was ankle deep. The bedroom was only slightly drier than the thatched hut, but we got under blankets and mosquito nets and made the best of the situation. It was a very ' damping ' experience, but it happened in the warmer weather and we suffered no ill effects from sleeping in wet blankets.

I have two sons now, both strong and healthy. Soon after the elder was born I was allowed into the room to see him and my wife. The baby was wrapped in swaddling clothes and laid on a table by the bedside. " Take a look at your son," said the nurse, unwrapping some coverings. I looked down and saw a queer little mite of humanity coloured blue and purple. " What an ugly little devil! " was my too unguarded comment. We named the boy ' Victor.' Had he been a girl he would have been called Victoria—to record our association with the Falls. The second son was born four years later, and as an infant he was not at all strong. When he was about seven we took him to a specialist in Johannesburg. This man's verdict was a grave one : that the boy's heart was weak and that he would not live to be ten years old. To-day this son is strong and healthy. I am sure that he owes his life to the unremitting care of his mother. He has been the supreme object of her devotion.

One never knew in those early days what the next moment would bring of excitement. Professor Henry Balfour of Oxford made an extended visit to the Falls in 1906, seeking for ancient implements of flint, and we got to know him well. I was able to show him a good place, about four miles from the Falls, where there were plenty of flint arrowheads, flint adzes, and other things of the sort. He discovered other places for himself, and got together a pretty collection of flint implements.

One night my wife and I were giving Professor Balfour dinner. During the meal a tin dish clattered loudly in the kitchen, but no remarks were made there or in the dining-room. When the house-boy was clearing away he remarked quite casually that a leopard had chased one of our fowls into the kitchen half-way through dinner. As he was going out of the dining-room he had seen the leopard departing one way from the kitchen and his wife another way. The fowl, he said, was still on the table. We went out to look, and it was there all right—apparently still petrified with fright. But if the hen and the boy and the boy's wife had got a scare, so had the the leopard. The fowl had knocked over the tin dish, and the clatter had made the big cat sheer off. I consider it odd, all the same, that the boy never thought to mention the happening until he had got through the routine of serving dinner, and then only casually. It was all, you see, very much in the day's work, however exciting or unexpected, and my wife faced every situation stoically.

In 1906 a rifle club was formed at Victoria Falls. We had a roster, to begin with, of about thirty members. A range was cut out in the bush and butts set up at ranges up to a thousand yards. Rifles were issued to us by the Government, and we were issued with ammunition at a cheap rate. Sunday was competition day, and target practice went on most weekdays. A visitor interested in shooting was for a time at the hotel, and one Sunday he came out with the club members to the range. He spent the morning with us, and was interested enough to offer us a silver cup for competition. The competition was to cover six months' shooting, the best score over a certain number of shoots to win the cup. Well, now. In 1906–7 the population at the Falls was more or less a transient one. The shooting went on, but some members got wanderlust, others were transferred to other parts. I was stationary. At the end of six months I was the only one of the members eligible for the cup, and I won it. Twenty-eight years after the event I had the donor's name engraved upon it: " The Freeman-Thomas Cup." Mr Freeman-Thomas is now a peer, but I cannot remember his title. If this should chance to catch his eye he may be amused to remember presenting the cup —and the circumstances in which it was won.

I would often go out for an afternoon with my shotgun after pheasants or guinea-fowl. One day, about three miles up the river, I got on to a bunch of guinea-fowl, but they rose before I was near enough for a shot. I followed them, and noted the spot where they had landed. I was not at all certain that I should get another chance at them, for they are great runners at times, and are apt to sprint far enough away from their landing-place.

I got near to the spot where I thought they might be, but saw nothing of them. I saw, however, about forty yards off, what I took to be a young pig moving through the bush. Up went my gun, and I let him have it. There was a yell, and a nigger jumped up in the air and disappeared again. This was my ' pig.' My aim had been all too true. I knew, of course, what had happened. This fellow with another couple had been out cutting grass for thatching, but instead of getting on with the job had been loafing in a *donga*, or ditch. Hearing me, they had cut for it, stooping low and running along the *donga* to get out of my sight, but the back of one of them hadn't been low enough. It had, in fact, been just at a height to be mistaken for a young pig.

I went along and found the shot native unconscious. His friends had disappeared towards the hotel farm about a mile and a half away, and a little later a negro with a crowd of others came on the scene to catch the white man who had shot a native. The natives knew me, and I had them carry the shot boy to the farm, where I did my best to patch him up. Also, I sent a lad off to Livingstone for a doctor. Then I set out for home accompanied by the hotel book-keeper, who had turned up at the farm on hearing that a murder had been committed. As we were walking back to the Falls I became aware that a couple of native police constables were walking behind me.

" What the deuce are you doing? " I demanded.

" We were told to bring you in to the police station,"
was the reply.

This got my goat. Native police are never sent to take
in a white. I became very angry.

" Get to blazes out of it ! " I yelled, " unless you want
to be shot ! "

They got.

Naturally I reported to the police. By the greatest of
good luck I was not asked to produce my shooting
licence. I hadn't one!

The event had curious effects. The hotel manager, for
example, heard that one of his pigs had been shot, and
he set off to the farm at breakneck speed on a bicycle.
On his way, however, he heard that it wasn't a pig but
a native that had been peppered, whereupon he lost
interest in the case and went back.

The doctor arrived at the farm and found that the boy
had suffered no great damage. The native hide is thick,
and at forty yards none of the shot had penetrated to
anything vital. But a lot of the shot were embedded just
under the skin. These the doctor did not attempt to
remove, and the back later showed a series of pimples,
as it were, where the shot had lodged. I didn't see the
doctor myself, and he sent me in no bill for his services,
but he told the tale with great gusto in Livingstone. For
a long time afterwards I could not visit that township
without being greeted derisively with loud questions:
" Who shot the pig? " and " What's the price of pork? "

It was a coincidence that the shot native's name was
' N'gulubu,' which means nothing other than ' pig.'
Hence most of the joking, and the hotel manager's
mistake. A month after the event I was standing in my

garden when a native walked in by the front gate. He was all a-grin. No natives were allowed to use that entrance, and I told him so. " Go round by the back! " I said. He still kept smiling broadly.

" I'm N'gulubu," says he.

" Oh, are you? " says I. " Well, here's ten bob for you."

He went off happily. Not only had he got two bob for the month he was laid off, wages for doing nothing, but he had ten bob on top of that. It must have been like the side of a house to N'gulubu. Everybody was satisfied, it seemed. Certainly I was. I had peppered two niggers at a cost of twelve shillings.

One evening towards sundown my wife, myself, and the sergeant of police were sitting in the garden when we heard the roar of a lion not far off. The sergeant and I decided we would go and look for it. We took rifles and set out. The roar of a lion is always difficult and elusive as a clue to his whereabouts, but we followed the direction of the sound to the best of our ability, and after a time we seemed definitely to locate it. It led us ultimately to the railway line where Lord Selborne's special train was parked. There we found our lion. It was a Zulu boy, attendant on the train, who with a primitive horn, his hands and breath, was giving a fine imitation of the lion's roar. The sergeant and I, at all events, had been properly taken in by it.

CHAPTER XVIII

UPS AND DOWNS

ABOUT 1907–8 I was elected a Fellow of the Royal Geographical Society. It was an honour that I greatly appreciated. I had Professor Balfour to thank for it, for it was he who secured my election. Later I made comparisons photographically with the sketches of the Falls made by Livingstone, Bain, and others. I took photographs from the same points as the sketches had been made from, and at the same time of day and month of the year. It was an interesting bit of work. The sketches by Bain were, I found, the most accurate. The results of the comparison I presented to the R.G.S.

By this time I had settled down to a sedentary life, more or less. I was married and knee-halted. There was no more roaming " wide and handsome " for me.

In 1908 I bought nine canoes from Canada, and also got a motor-launch. With these I started a boating business, and right from the start it was a good, money-making enterprise. All the bookings were made at the hotel—which belonged then, as now, to the Rhodesian Railway Company—and I paid the hotel a percentage. After a time I was approached by the general manager of the company with a view to the purchase of my boating business. As I refused to sell, the hotel bought a launch for itself. This cooked my goose, for, as I have said, all the bookings were made at the hotel office. I had about as much chance of carrying on in opposition

243

as I would have of coughing effectually against thunder. I just had to sell.

I now got another idea of making money, and I took a trip home on the strength of it. My notion was to run a trolley-line down to the bridge and the landing-stage. I was very kindly received at the B.S.A. Company's office in London Wall, but after exhibiting details of my scheme I was told that the whole thing was in the province of the railway company. Back at the Falls I saw one of the railway surveyors at the station. He was making inquiries about the very route I had suggested for a trolley-line. It was quite a coincidence. Then years went by, however, before the trolley-line came into being. I have always believed that I got the idea first, and believing that I think I ought to have shared the profit.

Balked of putting the trolley-line into operation, I searched for another idea for the transport of visitors to various points of interest about the Falls, and I hit on the notion of rickshaws. I imported a few of those vehicles, the first to appear about the Falls, and they became very popular indeed. I made a charge of half a crown for two persons to go together by rickshaw to the bridge or the boathouse—a charge which I think was eminently reasonable. A few months after my institution of this popular means of conveyance one of the higher officials of the railway turned up at the Falls, and he sent me a very peremptory notice requiring my immediate attendance upon him at the hotel. Now, I knew this official of old, and I did not like the tone of his message. I replied that I would look him up at my convenience, which would probably be in about an hour.

The hotel in those days was a wood and iron building, very warm, as I have said earlier, in summer and bitterly cold in winter. The manager's office was an apartment about ten feet by eight. When I went along to see the high-and-mighty official at my own time it was into this cubby-hole that I was invited for the interview. The official, I knew, was a non-smoker, and, as I say, I was not very fond of him. I put on my pipe at full blast and went into the cubicle. The high official started the interview in a very highly official, not to say autocratic, tone indeed.

" Mr Clark," he said, " I have sent for you regarding the rickshaws. Your prices are much too high. One shilling would be enough to charge either to the boats or to the bridge."

I poured out volumes of smoke from my pipe into the confined space of the cubicle.

" Mr ——," I asked, " are the rickshaws yours or mine? "

" Yours, of course," was the reply, " but you have got to charge one shilling either way."

There was nothing, of course, to allay my annoyance in his tone, and I did not bother to hide my feelings.

" My price is half a crown," I said, " and what authority have you, in any case, for laying down the law to me? "

He was a Welshman and very excitable. He fumed in more ways than one, for he was breathing thick smoke, and coughing to beat the band.

" I have advertised the price as one shilling," he blustered, " and that is the price you are going to charge! "

" I'll see you in Hades first," said I. " If you want to charge that price you had better buy the damned rickshaws! "

" How much do you want for them? "

I quoted a price, and he accepted it, glad to get out of the smother I had created into the fresh air. I was satisfied, but the manager of the hotel wasn't. He met me right afterwards and told me that I wouldn't have got the price out of him. I told him I knew that, but that the rickshaws were worth the money.

Up to the time that I sold the rickshaws it was the practice of my wife and myself to spend the afternoon at the boat landing-stage, a very pleasant spot. I would take my fishing-tackle, and while my wife sat sewing or that, with our son playing around, I would fish with live bait for tiger-fish or bream.

One afternoon I caught a tiger-fish of about a pound weight, and returned it to the river. The next afternoon I caught another tiger-fish of about a pound and did likewise. When I found myself catching a pound tiger-fish every afternoon I took the trouble to mark one of the gills. I had no sooner put him back than he was on my line again. It may sound a fisher's yarn, but in honest fact I caught that same fish forty-eight times by count. I failed, however, to reach the half-century with him. I can only suppose that some one else caught this willing biter and, not knowing his amazing willingness, took him home for a meal.

There was one afternoon when my line on casting got caught on a rock about twenty yards out. I called the rickshaw boy and told him to swim out and release the hook. The rock was just above the rapids. The boy got out to the rock all right, and dropped below the surface, but the hook still held. He dropped below the surface level once again, but, I could see, in an unnatural way. I took off my jacket and stuffed my watch and bacca into it—the bacca-pouch was merely a bag that I tucked into my belt. My wife entreated: " Don't go in. You will be drowned! " But I couldn't stand by and see the lad go down. There was nothing for it but to go in after him. In I went, boots and all. I reached the boy, but before I could get a grip on him he had me by the neck. By the time I freed myself I was pretty well exhausted. I managed to tow him half-way to the bank, but by then I was played out entirely. I got to the bank for a second or two's rest. He was drifting down to the rapids, so I went after him again. When I had got him within a yard or two of the bank again, I yelled to my wife : " For God's sake throw something in! " I meant a bit of wood or anything that would float. But, being excited, she grabbed the first thing handy and chucked it. This happened to be my jacket with my watch and bacca in the pockets. It didn't do much good either to me or the watch or the bacca, but I recognized that she did her best.

I managed to get the boy to land, and had to flatten out for a bit before starting in to get him round. He took it all as a matter of course, and I gave him a couple of bob for saving his life. I felt he deserved it.

Another afternoon still, but at the house this time, our native boy came and told me there was a snake on the stoep. I picked up the first stick that came to hand, and it chanced to be the butt of my fishing-rod. In the angle of the stoep walls I found a hooded cobra coiled up. It was very difficult to get a blow in where it lay. It put its head up and spread its hood as I struck at it. It was impossible to get in a clean stroke, and as I lashed at it with the rod-butt it spat into my eye. They say that a spitting snake seldom misses the eye. I was in immediate agony, but I managed to kill the reptile. The pain in my eye increased every second, and I was dancing all over the place with it. I sent off a boy to Livingstone for the doctor, but in the meantime asked among my labourers if any of them knew of a remedy. Natives, it is well known, have many useful and curious cures for the sicknesses and accidental injuries peculiar to the country. None of them, however, could suggest anything for taking the pain of the snake-spit from my eye till one very old boy turned up. He demanded a chopper and a large spoon. These he took to a tree that grew within fifty yards of the house. He made an incision in its bark and collected a spoonful of the sap. This he brought to me and told me to pour it into the eye. If he had given me sulphuric acid I think I would have obeyed him, the pain was so dreadful.

I put the sap into my eye as bidden, and it came out green. I kept on with the treatment, and the relief was immediate. By sundown the eye was fairly comfortable, and I had a good night's rest. Next day I kept a bandage over the eye, but the pain had quite gone. That day the boy got back from Livingstone with some drops the doctor had sent, but I never used them. There was no need. I have known of cases of snake-spit in the eye where the victims have been in the doctor's hands for two or three weeks before getting better. I told the doctor about it and advised him to take samples of the tree-sap. He looked at the tree, but I heard no more about it. I have often thought since that if I had only taken sap from the tree and isolated the active constituent, possibly in crystalline form, I should have had a very useful drug for the alleviation of pain in cases such as my own.

We wanted a native to work in the house, but natives for house-boys were scarce. I was at this time unable to get one locally, so I went over to Livingstone to seek for one of the right sort. All I could get was a big and hefty negro, who looked a really villainous character. But, I said to myself, one cannot always judge by looks—and I engaged him.

He started work next morning, and it soon became apparent that his looks in no way denied him. He was a rotter. He would not do anything my wife asked him to do, and was altogether very insubordinate, so I gave him a good hiding with the sjambok I always kept handy. The well-deserved thrashing only made him more sullen. Towards the approach of evening I came across a big puff adder. This is a very deadly snake, but sluggish of nature. Unlike other snakes it will not move out of the way of humans, but will wait to bite them. I was on the point of decapitating this specimen with a shovel, for they are the easiest snakes in the world to kill if you see them first, when the new boy begged me not to. He knew a man who bought snakes, and if I would let him capture it he could make a little trade. Having done what I conceived to be my duty by the boy, I had no ill feelings, so I let him box the snake and take it away.

As we retired that night and were entering the bed-room hut my wife saw a hand-towel lying on the floor just beyond the door. Her naturally tidy nature assert-ing itself, she stooped to pick the towel up. With it she picked up a snake, which, fortunately, was asleep at the moment. It was the puff adder that the boy had boxed and taken away. In revenge for the thrashing I had given him, he had brought it back after dark and left it on the bedroom floor. We never saw that boy again.

There was another time when I had to thrash a boy for giving cheek to his ' Missus.' I gave it to him good, because there was no use doing the thing by halves. I have always tried to be just, and have never given a boy a hiding unless he deserved it. This one deserved all he got, and he knew it. We never had a better boy than he was after the hiding. He stopped with us for years until we went home, and when we got back to the Falls he returned to our service. I say that a dog and a native are on a par. One should give them a good hiding when they really have earned it, but one should never thrash either until one's temper has cooled.

In 1916 Lord Buxton visited the Falls on his way to Katambora, forty miles up-river from Livingstone. I was appointed official photographer to accompany his Excellency. With the party were two future Governors of Southern Rhodesia: Captain Rodwell and Mr Herbert Stanley. Mr Stanley was afterwards knighted and appointed Governor of Northern Rhodesia, while later Captain Rodwell as Sir Cecil Rodwell became Governor of Southern Rhodesia. Still later Sir Herbert

Stanley was made High Commissioner for South Africa and, when Sir Cecil Rodwell's term of office expired, became Governor of Southern Rhodesia in his turn.

At Katambora Lord Buxton was to meet my old friend Litia of Sesheke, now Yeta III, Paramount Chief of the Barotse. The celebrations lasted three days, and after the formal meeting and Indaba were finished there were all sorts of festivities. Sports were held, and regattas in which scores of dug-outs participated. Shooting parties were organized, and angling for tiger-fish was favoured by many.

In 1918 came the great plague of what was called ' Spanish flu.' It is well known, of course, how this virulent type of influenza travelled the world over, in some parts wiping out whole families. It came to South Africa *via* Cape Town, and deaths were so numerous that practically all business was at a standstill. Carts travelled about the city collecting the dead. As the bodies could not all be buried they were simply taken to the beaches and left there to be washed away by the tide. These, at least, are the reports that came my way, and I can well believe them.

The epidemic spread like wildfire through the country, treating white and black folk alike, taking toll of all. Victoria Falls suffered with the other towns and settlements. For a fortnight not one train arrived from Bulawayo, there being neither engine-drivers nor fire-men to man the engines. We were isolated from the rest of the world. No provisions or vegetables came in from the south. Livingstone was in the like predicament. It had two doctors, one of them my old Irish friend the P.M.O. He was the first of the pair to go down, and his *confrère* went down also before the P.M.O. recovered. But my old friend dragged himself from his bed to attend to the now very sick population, a really heroic act. Those that were well worked day and night for their sick fellows, and it was a strenuous labour. It was notable that the big hefty fellows were the first to succumb.

At the Falls we had scarcely one well person. At the hotel, for example, the only person afoot of visitors and staff was the housekeeper. I was the only one in our household who was not down with the malady, and the sick included all our native servants, so that I had to look after all the invalids myself—my wife, both my sons, and the native servants. It was hard work. At one time my wife and our younger son were not expected to live. I had to nurse them night and day, making jellies from chicken and other materials, and barley water. For three nights I did not go to bed, but dozed in a deck-chair in snatches. I ate but little, for there was very little to eat. I kept myself going with stimulants.

When the epidemic was at its worst I had a visit from the hotel housekeeper. She came to me with the request that I would make chicken broth for the visitors and staff of the hotel who were down with 'flu. The request struck me as being a little thick, for the hotel had a big kitchen and one or two boys about on their feet, while I had my hands full as it was, with not a soul to help me. Still, I saw a funny side to the request, and the laugh did me good. I told the lady that if she would have the chickens sent over I would do the rest.

The doctor came once a week to visit the Falls from Livingstone by special train—the only train that ran—

SIR HERBERT STANLEY AND SIR CECIL RODWELL FISHING ON THE ZAMBESI

and he would send over Winchester quarts of medicine for everybody.

It was, as may be imagined, a miserable time. Fortunately I escaped the sickness and all my family recovered. As soon as they were able to travel I took them down to the coast—but there it was hardly more cheerful than elsewhere, the epidemic having passed through only a short while previously.

In 1919, Victor, our elder boy, was ten years old, but he had never been to school. Up to then he had been taught all he knew by his parents. He was well up in the three R's, but it was time he had some regular schooling. His mother did not like the idea of sending him away to a boarding school in the conditions then prevailing, so we decided to move to some place where he could go to school and live at home.

After long consideration we determined that the best plan would be to get into a business in a town, and leave a manager in charge of the Falls establishment for a year or two. By the end of that time Victor would be readier for sending to a boarding school. In pursuit of this idea, I advertised in the principal papers of Cape Colony and the Transvaal and Natal for a partnership in some well-established photographic business. I received many replies, and picked out one from Johannesburg. The name of the firm was well known to me as of good repute in the early days.

There were three partners in the business, which was registered as a limited liability company. The price seemed reasonable, and I made up my mind to buy a half share in the business if everything else was

satisfactory. I found a manager for the Falls establishment, a man I had known for a considerable time. We
packed our goods and chattels, and leaving the new
manager in charge, set out for Johannesburg.

The day after our arrival there I went to the studio of
the firm. It was situated in one of the busiest parts of
the town. Business seemed to be good, and the four
assistants to be fully occupied. I'll admit that I was
much too trusting and did not make all the inquiries I
should have. As a fact, I confined my inquiries to the
firm's book-keeper, and he was a new hand. Everything
seemed satisfactory in my innocent and unsuspecting
eyes, and I bought a half share in the business. Two of
the three members of the firm were to retire.

Houses could not be rented for love nor money, so,
after a month at a boarding-house, I found a suitable
house and bought it. The terms of purchase were so
much down, and the balance in monthly instalments,
covering the sum of one thousand pounds. It was a very
nice house, but it needed a coat of paint on its front.
This job I tackled myself. The attitude of our neighbours towards my activity was amusing. Apparently it
was the sort of thing ' not done ' in the neighbourhood,
and there were some upturned noses while I worked with
my paint-brushes on a Sunday morning. What my
neighbours thought, however, worried me none. I enjoyed the job, and saved a good deal of money by doing
it myself. I was excused, perhaps, for acting in a way
considered *infra dig.*, because I was, after all, a
Rhodesian. All Rhodesians other African provincials
believed to be half cracked.

To return, however, to the business I had **bought**

myself into. It wasn't long before I discovered that I had
been much too sketchy in my inquiries, that I had been
in fact Jimmy the Mug, and that I had been sold a pup.
The business was on its last legs, deeply in debt. I was
told later, indeed, that its creditors had been held off by
the tale that a rich man was coming into the business,
and that if I had not come in the firm would have been
made bankrupt.

Well, there the position was. I had expended all my
available capital in buying myself into this business, and
in purchasing a house which in itself was a burden of
debt to me. The more I saw of the actual state of affairs
the less hopeful I became. There was practically no
stock of chemicals or of printing material in the firm.
I therefore had to go out and buy what was needed.
I gave an order to a wholesale firm for a hundred-
weight of hypo, a supply of printing papers and other
materials, and everything was gay and hearty until I
mentioned the name of the firm and that I had pur-
chased a partnership in it. Then I got what is known as
the frozen mitt. I was told new supplies could hardly be
forthcoming until the firm's outstanding account had
been paid. Another shock was my discovery that money
which I had banked to the firm's credit was being drawn
upon by the original partners. I had not made any new
arrangement for the signing of the firm's cheques.

I had, indeed, been sold a pup, but there was nothing
I could do about it save carry on. I started to advertise
on a large scale, and contrived to attract a fair amount
of business, but the going was hard. Bills and old liabilities had to be met, and creditors, having experience
of the firm, were not inclined to be kind. I managed to

get along for a time, but at last my resources were exhausted. There was not only the business to carry; there was a supposedly active partner who was, in my view, no more than a passenger. He did not pull his weight. While I, who was doing all the work, did not ever draw my agreed salary from the business, he extracted his full whack every week. At the end of six months I was dead broke. There were times when I could not buy even a newspaper.

To add to my troubles, I contracted pneumonia, and was laid up for six weeks. It may be gathered that the situation was considerably worse when I got back into harness again.

One thing and another happened until it was evident to me that my partner was not only not pulling his weight, but was pulling against me. I went the length of confronting him before a lawyer and exposing his conduct in the hope that he would throw his hand in. In the end I saw that it was useless going on any longer. As things were, I would only get deeper into the hole. I had tried my best for eighteen months. I decided to liquidate the business and get back to Rhodesia, where I could make a decent living, so I called in a firm of chartered accountants and instructed them to wind up the business. I was myself the firm's biggest creditor on account of salary which I had been unable to draw. The business was sold, and the creditors were paid at the rate of seventeen shillings and sixpence in the pound. I sold my house for six hundred pounds, and got back to Rhodesia.

During the eighteen months I had been in Johannesburg I had been able only once to visit the Falls to see how things were going with my establishment there. I had received some money monthly from the business, otherwise I could not have kept pegging along in Johannesburg.

In my absence I had given my power of attorney to a friend in Bulawayo who visited the Falls periodically. On my return to Rhodesia I went into accounts with him, and found to my dismay that I owed some seven hundred pounds, mostly in Bulawayo. I made a round of my creditors.

The first I interviewed was one to whom I owed two hundred and seventy pounds. I was greeted cordially. I said at once: " I owe you a lot of money, and I can't pay you. What is my position with regard to your firm? What steps do you intend to take? "

" None at all," was the answer. " None now, that is, Mr Clark—though I had the intention. I have written to your manager repeatedly, but got no reply from him. If you hadn't turned up, I should have put him through it, and you would have been in the bankruptcy court within the next month."

I had dealt with this firm for many years, and what was said then put me just on top of the world. Notwithstanding my unfortunate position in owing so much money, I felt very proud—and very humble.

" Mr Clark," said this creditor, " now that you are back, I need not worry. I know that you will pay me. You can have anything you need for carrying on, and you can pay me when you like."

I could have wept. It was almost worth while being so broke to hear such words from a man to whom I owed so much.

I went the round of my creditors and, with one exception, all were equally kind. The exception was a man in Livingstone. I made a point of seeing him as soon as I could on my return to the Falls. I owed him thirty pounds. I explained my position and asked to be supplied with five pounds' worth of goods to carry on with in my general store. He said that my order was too small, and that he did not supply retail.

A fortnight later I went into his store with an order. He refused to supply me, asking me when I was going to pay his account.

" How much do I owe you? " I asked.

He called his book-keeper and bade him bring Mr Clark's account. When the book-keeper returned, the merchant asked : " How much does Mr Clark owe us? "

" Nothing," the book-keeper replied. I had paid my debt before asking any further credit from the firm.

" All right! " said the proprietor. " Mr Clark can have what he wants."

" You can go to hell! " I said. " You'll never get another order from me! "

And though for many years after he sent me a catalogue yearly, I never did deal with him again.

On returning to Rhodesia our son Victor went to the Milton School in Bulawayo. Of his stay there I have one story to relate. The boy had to wear spectacles. One vacation, when on our way down to the coast we had picked him up by arrangement, we saw that he was not wearing them, and we asked him where they were. He must have left them at school, he said, and volunteered no further information. We could not replace the spectacles just then, not having the oculist's prescription with us. It was not until a year later that we learned what had happened. Mr Hickson, the noted faith-healer, had been visiting Bulawayo and had effected some wonderful cures there. Victor and a friend had gone to Mr Hickson, and as a result had discarded their spectacles. To this day neither boy has found any need to wear glasses again. My wife and I know the relatives of our son's friend, and they confirmed the story absolutely.

CHAPTER XIX

WE CARRY ON

L IFE at the Falls remains full of interest to this day. It will be everlastingly full of event.

In 1925 the Prince of Wales (the present King Edward) paid us a visit, and my wife and I, as the oldest residents, had the honour of presenting his Royal Highness with an ivory cigarette case. We had it made from a solid piece of native ivory, with an inlaid inscription in gold, " Victoria Falls, 1925."

In that same year I was elected an Associate of the Royal Photographic Society. Before that time I was a mere Member. I consider the Associateship a great honour, particularly because I was among the first fifty to become Associates in the whole of Africa from the Cape to Cairo. My ambition is to become a Fellow, a much greater honour. I have tried twice to attain this, unsuccessfully. I have not lost hope, however, but will try again.

On three occasions after my return from Johannesburg I was asked to become a Justice of the Peace, and each time refused on the ground that to accept would have meant a financial loss I could ill afford. I was recruiting labour for the tobacco plantations in the south, and the contracts for certain periods had to be signed by a Native Commissioner, a Magistrate, or a Justice of the Peace. I could not very well engage labour and at the same time sign contracts as a J.P. I had to make a choice between recruiting or accepting the honour. I needed the two pounds per head I was receiving for the natives I engaged, and had to decline.

I might well say a word here of my establishment at the Victoria Falls. The curio store is a thatched hut on a native model, and the general store is built of old railway sleepers. The psychology of customers has to be studied, and I find that this primitive architecture intrigues our visitors. But I cannot do better, as a description of my business, than quote the following account of it from an English newspaper:

> The Store itself is merely a thatched hut, fourteen feet in diameter, in a style typical of the African native. It is the establishment of Mr Percy M. Clark, A.R.P.S., F.R.G.S., F.R.E.S., at the Victoria Falls. Entering (a tall person has to stoop a bit), there is disclosed in the centre a large table on which are displayed curios from all parts of Africa; ivory and ebony curios from Nyassaland, bead and grass work from Tanganyika, carved elephant-tusks from the Congo, native carvings and trays from Barotseland, native work of snake and iguana skins, wooden and clay models from all parts of Central Africa, crude models of ivory, teak, and ebony. Here also is to be seen a Devil's mask taken from the West Coast of Africa seventy years ago, and hanging from the wall is a priest's symbol of the Phallic worshippers brought from the Lower Congo. A very rare specimen, this is a most interesting article, as it must have worked down from Egypt during centuries.
>
> On the door hangs a weird figure which is Mr Clark's juju. This foisted itself on him many years ago. Ugly as sin, nobody has ever attempted to steal it, except one man, and he is dead.
>
> Round the hut on a circular table one sees post cards, photographs, etc. Also roll films, ciné films, photos of natives and native life, taken nearly forty years ago when natives were clothed mostly in sunshine, witch doctors, and warriors of the Matabele. There are photographs of Rhodes choosing

his grave site in the Matoppos, and of Alan Wilson who with his command was massacred at Shangani in 1896. On the monument near Rhodes' grave is the simple inscription: " There were no survivors."

Mr Clark calls himself a photographic artist, but, as he says himself, he isn't really. He takes photos and sells them, which is the principal thing.

(Enter a Customer)

" Please give me a film."

" Madam, you are an optimist."

" Why? "

" I sell films, madam."

" Two Number 120's, please."

" I thank you! "

(Along comes the next)

" You don't sell ciné films, do you? "

" Sir, first you tells a lie, then you axes a question. I do."

Lots of fun with customers. The environment is so different from an ordinary shop. Just a hut, no counter, and the curiosity of the customers establishes pleasant relations at once. As the customer walks in, one hears: " Isn't that quaint! " and then: " Is this a Kaffir kraal? " " No, sir. This is a respectable establishment." " Oh, I beg your pardon! " " Don't mention it, the pleasure is mine." And so it goes on.

A Royal lady came along one day incog. " Mr Clark, can I rootle round? " " Certainly, Madam." As her Royal Highness comes to some clever clay models of monkeys, the question is asked: " Mr Clark, where do these come from? " " Well, Madam—these monkeys are caught in the Rain Forest and petrified under the Falls. You can always tell when they are ripe because their tails drop out—and then I sell them for two shillings." H.R.H. looked sideways and her eyes twinkled, but questions *re* monkeys were left in abeyance.

Having a sense of humour and also the ridiculous, Mr Clark quite enjoys life. All sorts and conditions of the human species pay him a visit, and, though life is quiet, it is seldom dull. Many celebrities have visited his modest establishment.

The last line quoted is most true. Colonel Frank Rhodes spent many hours with me when visiting the Falls, and we talked over old times in Rhodesia. The late King of the Belgians when Crown Prince came along, and we chatted for half an hour. His was a charming personality.

The Duchess d'Aosta, a cousin of the King of Italy, paid me a visit. She was seated outside my hut when she saw Victor playing in the garden. Victor was then about two years old. " Oh ! " the Duchess exclaimed. " I must give the darling a kiss ! " And she started towards him. But Victor had other ideas and ran away. Her Highness chased him all over the garden and finally caught him and kissed him, much to Victor's disgust.

Princess Marie Louise has visited the Falls two or three times, and on each occasion came to ' The Huts.' A charming lady, very homely in her ways. On her last visit she paid us the compliment of coming to our drawing-room, also a hut, to have a chat and a cigarette. I think she enjoyed her informal visit as much as we did. Incidentally, her cigarette-holder seemed to be just under a yard long.

Sir Charles Coghlan, the first Prime Minister of Southern Rhodesia, I knew in the early days. Kindly, genial, and always ready to be interested in other people, he is always the same, eager with advice and sympathy. The last time I met him we travelled together from the Falls to Livingstone in the guard's van of a goods train.

I must not forget to mention an uncrowned queen who visited me. Her husband was the Chewing-gum King of the New World. She came over with a boatload of

Americans, and they owned the Falls for a few days. Chewing-gum was in demand, and I got some for the store. The lady came in with a big bunch of her friends, and almost the first thing she saw was the gum. " Say, folks! " she exclaimed delightedly. " Look here—get a load of this! Our gum, right here in the heart of Africa —right here at Victoria Falls! Isn't it a thrill, folks? I must tell Jawn, and take some home with me! " And she did, too. I feel certain she got more thrill out of the encounter than she did out of our wonderful scenery at the Falls.

One day, there being a goodly number of people in my hut, an American among them picked up a copy of my *Guide to the Victoria Falls*. Turning over the pages he came on the line which reads: " The bridge was built by the Cleveland Bridge Company, Darlington, England." Evidently he didn't read farther than the actual name of the Company, because he began to expound on the marvel of the bridge, and how it, being the most wonderful bridge in the world, could not have been built by anyone but Americans. I let him enthuse for quite a while along this line, then interrupted gently. " Excuse me, the bridge was not built at Cleveland, Ohio, but by the Cleveland Bridge Company of Darlington in England. It was designed and erected by a British firm." For a moment or two he was completely nonplussed, but at last jerked out: " Well—it's a vurry fine bridge! " And he got out of the hut.

Not so very long ago I saw a lady and gentleman stop dead on entering by the gate to my huts. When I came up to them they said hastily: " Don't go in! There's a leopard inside! "

264

" Nonsense! " I said. " I've been sitting here for quite
a time, and I've seen no leopard. Let's have a look! "

I went inside, but there was no leopard. I mildly suggested that they should take more water with it.

" But we saw it go in! " they insisted.

Once again I went in and searched the hut. Lifting
up the *limbo*, I saw a huge iguana. I promptly laid it
out with a knobkerry. I've seen many strange things
mistaken for a leopard, but nothing stranger than
that.

When Mr Leo Weinthal started *The African World*
I was appointed correspondent for the paper at Victoria
Falls. Since then I have done a good deal of Press work
for various papers and agencies. I am correspondent for
Reuter's, *South Africa*, the Exchange Telegraph Company, London, *Bulawayo Chronicle*, *The Star* of Johannesburg, *The Natal Weekly Advertiser* of Durban, and
my home paper, *The Cambridge Chronicle*. I also write
articles here and there.

At times it was just as well that I had other activities
than those centring in my huts. Foot-and-mouth disease
broke out in Southern Rhodesia, and for two and a half
years native curios were not allowed out of the country.
If this was not enough to affect our livelihood, there was
a monetary problem also. South Africa was on the gold
standard, and we were on sterling in Rhodesia. This
meant that our pound had the exchange value of eleven
shillings. The area affected by the foot-and-mouth
disease was some four hundred miles away from the
Falls, and it seemed farcical to prevent the export of
curios from a place such a distance away. What was
still more farcical was that when at last our goods could

go out because Southern Rhodesia was free, the disease was rife in Northern Rhodesia, only sixty miles from us.

In 1928 I went through a bad experience. For some months I had had a pain, a very localized pain in my stomach, and week by week I had gradually got weaker. I said nothing about it for a long time, but at last I had to confess I was not feeling at all well. Still, however, I did not seek medical advice. I thought the thing would pass off. Then as time went on I found myself unable to keep down my food. The slightest exertion brought on pain and utter exhaustion. I could not even shave without sitting down to rest two or three times during the process.

One Sunday evening towards sundown while I was walking from one hut to another I fell flop on my face, making noises like a hen with membranous croup. I got up with difficulty and went to bed. At least, I got on top of my bed with my clothes on. My wife and my son, it so happened, had friends in for the evening, and I made an effort to get up and join them, but I could not manage it. After a time my wife came along to see me; I protested that I was all right, or fairly all right, and she was not to upset the party. After a time she left me alone. Then I decided to get into bed, but I found that I had not got the strength to get out of my clothes. At long last the party broke up, and I was put to bed. Even then I would not hear of the doctor being sent for.

In the morning I just had to give in. The doctor was 'phoned for, and came along about four in the afternoon, not being told of any urgency.

He made a careful examination. " Good God! " he

exclaimed. "You haven't a drop of blood in your body!"

Not to make a long story of it, I'd been having internal hæmorrhages for months. I was very seriously ill, so seriously ill, in the doctor's opinion, that the only frail chance I had of surviving was to get to hospital in Livingstone straight away. If I stopped at home I should be dead in two days, he declared. If I attempted to reach Bulawayo for a better opinion, I should die on the way. That night I was put, bed and all, into a goods train and taken to Livingstone.

My wife wrote home, preparing our respective families for the worst. But, being stubborn, I refused to pass out as expected. I am not of a worrying nature. For a whole week, I think it was, I was not allowed one drop of liquid refreshment. I was told not even to swallow my saliva. Only by promising faithfully that I would not engorge a single drop was I permitted to rinse out my mouth with water. It was, you see, touch and go for me, but obviously no tragedy—since I am still here to tell the tale.

Several months later, a week before Christmas, to be exact, I found that hæmorrhage had begun again. From my previous experience I knew that this was not necessarily immediately fatal, so I said nothing about it. I wanted to do nothing that would interfere with our Christmas and New Year festivities, which are rather more important with us than with most families, for we have three birthdays to celebrate between Christmas and the New Year.

On New Year's day I told my wife what had happened, and went over to the post office with intent to get in touch with the doctor by one of the only two 'phones we had at the Falls, the other being at the hotel. But on the way I met the doctor himself. He took the news very gravely, and came back with me to the huts. There was no doubt about it; he recommended that I should go to England to be operated on, and meantime he put me to bed. In later consultation with my wife and myself, however, he allowed that I might get the operation done in Johannesburg.

Came a day, as they used to say on the films, when I was put on a stretcher and taken to the train. The staff on the train looked after me splendidly, and fresh milk was waiting for me at Bulawayo. At Johannesburg I was conveyed to my lodgings in an invalid chair. I was too weak to be operated on immediately, and for a few days I was stall-fed to build me up for the ordeal. I'll cut out a lot I might tell about nine doctors fussing round me with X-rays and what not, and merely say that I was ultimately turned inside out for the removal of a duodenal ulcer, my appendix, and for short-circuiting— if that process is understood when so badly put.

When I recovered consciousness, after two days, I found a sausage-like bandage *sewn* to my tummy over a foot-long cut. I was lying on my back with my knees over a bolster, and in this position I remained for days, not allowed to move. The knee-bolster was called a ' donkey '; after a few days it was removed, and I could move a little.

" I see," said the Sister that night, when she came in to take up her duty, " that you've lost your donkey! "

As evidence that I was not ' down and out ' I attempted a feeble joke.

THE OLD-TIMER

" Not a bit of it, Sister," I replied, " not while you're about! "

Next night she gave my wife a laugh by getting back at me. She was just leaving after her usual visit.

" Is there anything I can do for you? " she asked.

" Yes, Sister," I said, " you can kiss me ' Good night! ' "

" No, thanks! " she flashed back. " I leave all the rough-stuff to the orderlies! "

In less than three weeks I asked the surgeon if I might return to Rhodesia. He ran the tape over me, so to say, and said that I was a marvel, that he had never seen such a quick recovery, and that I could go when I liked. The operation was worth the four hundred quid it cost me altogether, for since it I have been a new man, full of health and as fit as a fiddle. Once again I was made aware of the depths of human kindness, and gladdened by the manifestations of friendship that my peril evoked. My Johannesburg landlady, for example, was kindness itself. She visited me in hospital before I went to the table, and I heard later that on her way she had gone to church to put up a special prayer for my recovery. I am sure it helped, that prayer, for she was a good woman, and—the prayer of the just availeth much.

That last Johannesburg adventure did not, apparently, age me. Only the other day a man came into my store. He had, he said, been at the Falls twenty-five years earlier, and had met my father.

" That's odd," I replied. " My father has been dead for fifty years."

" He wasn't at the Falls twenty-five years ago? "

" No. It must have been myself you met."

"Well," said my visitor, "I wouldn't have believed it! The man I met seemed older than you are now!"

Quaint things still happen in my place. Hanging up in my curio store there is a photograph, taken by me thirty-one years ago, of an old prospector whom I met at the Falls; it is very typical of the early days in Rhodesia. There are very, very few of his type left to-day. The picture has been exhibited in the United States and other countries and bears the legend: 'The Old-timer.' The prospector, who rejoiced in the good old Anglo-Saxon name of Bill Smith, had walked three hundred and fifty miles from the north, and I had footed it from Wankie in the south.

Two weeks ago, calculated from the day on which I sit writing this, a lady and a gentleman with two grown-up daughters came into the store. The ladies were examining the curios when the husband said quietly to his wife: "Look, my dear, there is a portrait of your father!" The lady took no notice. She was much too interested in the curios to hear. As they were preparing to leave the man again drew his wife's attention to the photograph. "Your father," he said. "Why, so it is!" the lady exclaimed.

There was, of course, a good deal of excitement over the discovery, and I was bombarded with questions. I told them of my meeting with the subject of the photograph. "That," I said, "is a portrait of old Bill Smith, and I haven't seen him from that day to this."

I was informed that my sitter's name was not 'Bill,' but 'Arthur.' The daughter did not possess a photograph of her father; I produced a spare copy, and she went away delighted.

I had better close my narrative with that odd echo from the past. If I recovered on the operation table at Johannesburg a large measure of the toll of health that Africa had exacted from me in my pioneering days, I realize nevertheless that I am not so young as I used to be. I long for another trip to the Old Country, which I have not seen for twenty-three years, and I am conscious that I am passing into the Autumn of my days—perhaps the Winter. But putting one thing atop of the other, I have had something worth while out of life, vivid experiences to look back upon. I have seen a country pass out of savagery into civilization. Where once one might hump one's blankets and walk into the unknown, there is no unknown any more. Where once one might only tramp toilsomely, gaining a few poor miles a day, the motor-car speeds, while overhead the aeroplane covers a month's march in an hour. There is little romance left in Africa.

I have seen at the ' movies ' pictures of the once shy and unapproachable Pigmy tribes of the Congo riding in motor-trucks. I have seen pictures of the terrible dangers encountered by camera-men in the heart of Africa. Well, it may be that African life is of vast interest to the peoples who frequent the picture palaces in the towns and cities of a closer packed, more industrial civilization than ours. Africa, it is true, has still much to offer of interest and beauty to the visitor, even of the greatest sophistication. A great noise in my ears reminds me that just over the way from where I write the Victoria Falls, if more approachable than when they first burst on my entranced vision, still keep in all essentials their unchangeable loveliness. This is what

271

Africa holds out to newcomers to-day, her vast and un-changing beauties, of which the Falls are but a single phenomenon. As for that rough-and-ready existence, that pioneering life which this—I am all too conscious—quite inadequate yarn has attempted to picture for you —well, let an ' Old Drifter ' greet all expectations of meeting it to-day with an amused, contented chuckle.